The Environmental Toolkit for Teachers

First Steps to Sustainability

Neil Fraser

Illustrations by Hanna Forsgren

B L O O M S B U R Y
LONDON • NEW DELHI • NEW YORK • SYDNEY

Published 2014 by Bloomsbury Education
Bloomsbury Publishing plc
50 Bedford Square, London, WC1B 3DP

www.bloomsbury.com

Bloomsbury is a registered trade mark of Bloomsbury Publishing Plc

9781441153012

1 3 5 7 9 10 8 6 4 2

Typeset by Fakenham Prepress Solutions, Norfolk, NR21 8NN
Printed by CPI Group (UK) Ltd, Croydon, CR0 4YY

This book is produced using paper that is made from wood grown in managed, sustainable forests. It is natural, renewable and recyclable. The logging and manufacturing processes conform to the environmental regulations of the country of origin.

To view more of our titles please visit www.bloomsbury.com

Contents

Acknowledgements

The author would like to thank Ian and Ann Fraser, Hanna, Ken, Callum, Mary Jane, Andrew and Julie Cunningham, Emily, Andreas, Susan and Jörn. Your time, encouragement and inspiration were greatly appreciated.

A further thanks to Stephen Bowkett and The Carbon Trust.

For those about to make the world a better place, we salute you.
For Mum, Dad and Paul

Introduction

Welcome to *The Environmental Toolkit for Teachers: First Steps to Sustainability,* the essential book to help you reduce the ecological footprint of your school. Schools have significant impacts on the environment and so have been tasked by the UK government with being sustainable by the year 2020 as part of the national strategy to reduce carbon emissions and create more sustainable communities. Individual teachers have been given the role of Eco-Teacher (sometimes referred to as Eco-Coordinators), and are expected to turn their schools into environmentally sustainable entities. Rather than being a burden, this expectation provides schools with an opportunity to involve their pupils in genuine action learning. Through active involvement in sustainability projects, pupils from across the entire school can create change now, while also developing the knowledge, skills and values that will help them to thrive in a future that looks increasingly complex and uncertain. However, to embed an ethos of environmental sustainability takes time and requires expertise in the application of various tools. Many Eco-Teachers that I've met simply have not had the time, knowledge or ideas to involve pupils in making a significant reduction to the school's ecological footprint and so I decided to create a 'toolkit' that solves these problems and provides Eco-Teachers with information and ideas that:

- Make best use of the time given to do eco-work.
- Help encourage a better understanding of the principles and practice of school environmental management.
- Set out fun and educational eco-projects.
- Provide opportunities to practise active citizenship with pupils.
- Save research time by listing the most helpful resources.
- Promote Eco-School status.

With those goals in mind, the book explains the principles of environmental management, the field of behaviour change and the workings of the Eco-Schools programme, as well as acting as a step-by-step guide to implementing litter, waste and energy projects with children.

School environmental management is mostly about planning and implementing systems and routines and the book shows how you, the Eco-Teacher, can take the lead on projects and coordinate the actions undertaken by the pupils, so that the tasks are done effectively while the children are given responsibility – a key element of active citizenship and enterprise education.

The Eco-Team is the term used for the group of people leading environmental work in the school and is usually led by one teacher, the Eco-Teacher. The Eco-Pupils are pupils from across the school dedicated to attending meetings and carrying out most of the routine tasks. Also in the team there may be the caretaker, a parent or another interested party such as a representative from the local council environmental department. The team can work independently of each other but come together at meetings to plan and discuss action.

How to use the book

The book is divided into four chapters. Chapter 1 covers the principles and background to creating an Eco School. Chapters 2, 3 and 4 cover three topics: litter, waste and energy. Each topic contains several projects, and within each project there are a number of actions that follow the principles explained in the theoretical part of the book. The actions are numbered so as to provide a logical order and are assigned to either the whole Eco-Team or just the Eco-Teacher or the Eco-Pupils. Many of the projects involve the whole school in a campaign, usually after the Eco-Team has put the systems and procedures in place. During such campaigns classroom teachers can spread the message throughout the whole school and deliver 'Supporting Classroom Lessons' to provide the knowledge and understanding to pupils not involved in the Eco-Team.

To successfully create an environmentally sustainable school relies on individuals and teams taking the initiative to take action, finding the time to do it and measuring and evaluating if the action is having the desired impact.

Taking action

After the principle and theory in Chapter 1, the following chapters focus on taking action. These chapters are list the projects and step-by-step actions for the Eco-Team to take. Within many of the projects there is an element of classroom teaching to engage pupils in the issues and deepen their understanding as to why the environmental management systems are being implemented.

Projects can be ongoing and engagement and encouragement should be continuous. However, a new focus for each term is recommended in order to keep the Eco-Team enthused. Most of the projects listed in this section can be undertaken at any time of the year and several can perhaps run concurrently. Different Eco-Team members or classes can be given responsibility for running the initiatives, but be aware that taking on too much at once can overstretch the focus and potentially divert interest from the element of monitoring and evaluating the systems.

Time

Often projects are ignored because of the perceived amount of time and work involved, but *many hands make light work*. Many of the tasks need not take long, especially as the project steps are laid out in this book and are quick and easy to follow. The Eco-Teacher can lead projects but the Eco-Pupils should carry out many of the tasks which not only forms part of their education but also saves the Eco-Teacher time. The remainder of the school pupils, classroom teachers, other staff and parents can all be involved. The steps within each project indicate who is best placed to carry out the task as in Table 1.

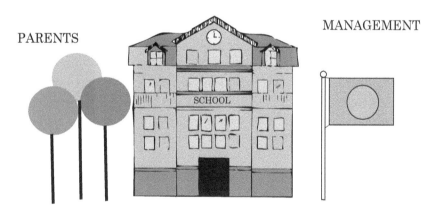

Whole-school sustainability involves many people working together.

Table 1 General responsibilities

Task leader	General responsibilities
Eco-Teacher	Environmental manager
	Meeting senior staff
	Training colleagues
	Discussions with outside agencies
	Coordinating projects
	Chairing Eco-Team meetings
Eco-Pupils	Environmental management action
	Daily/weekly collecting, monitoring, recording, evaluating data
	Raising awareness by engaging and informing classmates
	Leading assemblies
	Making posters and signs
	Attending and note-taking at Eco-Team meetings
Eco-Team (Eco-Teacher, Eco-Pupils, Others)	Eco-Teacher and Eco-Team meet
Class teachers	Exemplifying sustainable behaviour
	Teaching sustainability lessons and projects
Pupils	Exemplifying sustainable behaviour
	Learning about sustainability by taking part in assemblies and class lessons
	Getting parents involved
Caretaking staff	Supporting eco-initiatives
	Attending Eco-Team meetings
Kitchen staff	Supporting eco-initiatives
	Attending Eco-Team meetings
Senior management	Supporting eco-initiatives
	Approving budget for eco-initiatives
Parents	Supporting eco-initiatives
Outside agencies	Supporting eco-initiatives
	Supplying resources

Allocating these tasks among the Eco-Team and the whole school frees time for the Eco-Teacher and allows more people to become involved and engaged in the initiatives.

Monitoring and evaluating

Gauging the impact of any eco-initiative is an important aspect of environmental management but is sometimes poorly done. The Eco-Team should ensure that they undertake this element of their eco-work and record it as evidence for Eco-School accreditation.

So, when planning to undertake a project, follow each action step for the most effective results. Even if you have already covered a project or it is under way, review the system in place and see if it can be improved according to the plan suggested. Research is emerging to show the wider benefits of engagement in education for sustainability for pupils and schools. Children develop a broad range of skills, such as team-working, research, presentation, problem-solving, creative and thinking and systems thinking through their involvement in programmes such as Eco-Schools. Schools have also witnessed improvements in behaviour and wellbeing as children participate in projects they find engaging and stimulating. Values such as care, kindness, respect, cooperation and compassion are also activated and reinforced through involvement in sustainability projects. By capturing and reporting on these wider benefits Eco-Teams can strengthen the case for greater investment in education for sustainability. When designing and delivering projects be mindful of the knowledge, skills and values that will be developed, do your best to ensure they are being well developed and remember to record and report on them as much as possible.

Creating a sustainable school can be challenging and there will be barriers to overcome, so there are case studies to help learn from other schools and reading these will help you plan a realistic vision for your school. There is much that can be achieved if you and the pupils use the tools in this book to help your school take the first steps towards sustainability.

Good luck!

1 Why become an Eco-School?

Setting the context

By 2050 the global population will reach 10 billion all of whom will be striving to live healthy, fulfilling and peaceful lives. To achieve this many challenges will need to be overcome. Pressure on natural resources and the impacts of climate change and biodiversity loss will continue to intensify adding more complexity to a set of challenges the next generation will not only need to cope with, but also overcome. Today's schools need to prepare the next generation for the uncertain future that is emerging in front of them.

To educate is to develop the knowledge, skills and values needed to ensure today's children grow up to be active citizens with the ability to take us from where we are now, to where we need to be. Schools today need to ensure that the education they deliver is education for, rather than against, sustainability.

The need for reducing schools' ecological footprints comes from overwhelming evidence of global warming and climate change. The Earth's atmosphere is heating up and there is little doubt that man has contributed to this change by burning fossil fuels and releasing too much carbon dioxide into the air. Scientists say that we must reduce this output or be faced with a global average temperature that could seriously affect the way we live. A fuller explanation of climate change for teachers and pupils can be found at http://www.metoffice.gov.uk/education.

The UK government is committed to reducing national carbon emissions by 60% of 1990 levels by the year 2050 and schools must contribute by cutting their emissions at similar or better levels with much of this action needed now, or at least before 2020. Schools in the UK are, in fact, responsible for contributing 9.24 million tonnes of greenhouse gases into the atmosphere per annum[1] (1.3% of the total UK emissions), and so every school should be attempting a 30% to 50% reduction in its own emissions in the next few years if the education sector is to

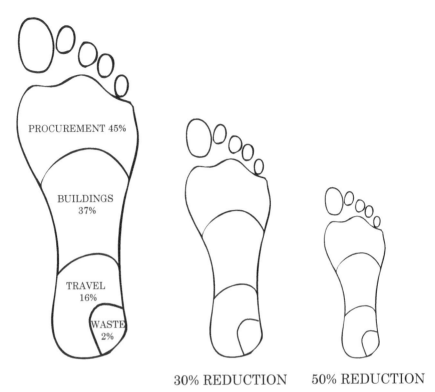

PROCUREMENT 45%

BUILDINGS
37%

TRAVEL
16%

WASTE
2%

30% REDUCTION   50% REDUCTION

Sources of carbon emissions in a typical school and reductions needed (figures from the Sustainable Development Commission, 2008)

succeed in making a significant difference. Each school should measure its own footprint and begin to implement the projects and strategies that bring about the culture change required. It is through the implementation of these projects, as a whole school, that education for sustainability can happen. By actively engaging children in designing and running environmental management systems schools can work simultaneously on the twin aims of lowering their ecological footprint and embedding education for sustainability across their formal and informal curriculum's. The Eco-Schools framework is designed to help them do both.

A need for societal change has been recognised, leading to the creation of the UK government Strategy for Sustainable Development, the Climate Change Act 2008 and the setting of targets to reduce carbon emissions as well as a plan for how to achieve them. This includes a plan for sustainable schools with the Department for Education setting itself six priorities (see the archives of the Sustainable Development Commission website at http://www.sd-commission.org) summarised as:

• Implementing the Carbon Reduction Strategy.

- Setting up a regulatory framework to encourage schools to improve learning outcomes on sustainability.
- Having more focus on sustainability in the curriculum.
- Enabling teachers and staff to lead sustainability in schools.
- Creating a vision of a sustainable school.
- Giving a higher profile to sustainability.

The government has decided upon an approach to its school estate and has begun plans for zero carbon schools, set out in the 'Road to Zero Carbon: Final Report of the Zero Carbon Task Force' publication. Agencies, such as the Sustainable Schools Alliance (http://se-ed.co.uk/edu/sustainable-schools/) and Sustainability and Environmental Education (http://se-ed.co.uk/edu), will attempt to help deliver the strategy by engaging with schools and communities to create a sustainability curriculum.

This sustainability strategy also involves communities taking more responsibility for their environment and it is the local primary school where community planners hope that sustainability projects will take root. Primary schools – at the heart of many communities – are well placed to engage the community and help spread the eco-message.

Economics is another context that drives the strategy for Eco-Schools. Local authorities are faced with rising energy costs and landfill tax and need to find ways to reduce expenditure. Sustainable schools spend less money as energy bills are lower and generate less waste meaning reduced landfill tax – appealing to cost-conscious local authorities. Council environmental departments are, therefore, keen to help schools find ways to cut costs and the Eco-Schools environmental management programme is one way to do it.

Contextual facts

Climate

- There has been a 0.75 degree increase in global temperatures in the last century.[2]
- The UK sea level has risen 10cm since 1900.[3]
- Almost 2% of total UK carbon emissions come from schools.[4]

Social

- Teaching active citizenship is statutory in schools.

COMMUNITY   EDUCATION AUTHORITY   SCIENTIFIC COMMUNITY

Those who influence sustainable school policy

- Funds such as the Big Lottery Communities Living Sustainably Fund and the Climate Challenge Fund are providing millions of pounds and supporting hundreds of communities.

Financial

- UK schools could reduce energy costs by £44 million.[5]

These contexts have come together to put schools at the forefront of social change and a new culture is slowly taking shape evident in the increase in participation of the Eco-Schools programme. Involvement in this initiative demonstrates that a school is committed to sustainability by having an environmental management system in place and will have completed a whole-school environmental review. Pupils and staff will have adopted many 'green' behaviours (see *Appendix 1* for a list of key sustainable behaviours); active citizenship, sustainability and enterprise will be integral to the ethos of the school and there will be community involvement. The Eco-Schools programme aids the drive for sustainability and provides a framework in which to conduct the projects and strategies in this book; but at present only 1700 schools in England have reached the prestigious Green Flag status.[6] In order to increase this figure and create more Eco-Schools that can truly be called sustainable, some changes in how schools operate and how teachers work are required. More robust and rigorous measures need to be taken if eco-strategies and projects are to be as effective as possible, and more pupils need to be fully engaged and given creative, exciting and motivating projects and tasks.

Teachers must be given time to do their eco-work and to learn more about environmental management by, for example, reading relevant texts, meeting and sharing information with other Eco-Teachers and attending relevant training courses. They also require a team they can delegate work to, funds to buy the relevant tools and resources and they also need to link up with communities in joint projects that spread the sustainability message.

These needs are placed on a backdrop where time is short. Creating a sustainable ethos does not happen overnight; green behaviours take time to take effect and some of the bigger changes that are required – such as changing heating systems – are costly and unaffordable to the single school. Local authorities can help, but they have tight budgets and finding funds to support sustainability projects may be difficult. However, low-cost everyday eco-actions in schools can reduce overheads and, at the same time, influence positive environmental attitudes.

Schools are pivotal to change and can play their part in many contexts. Social change is happening, Eco-School awards are rising and the green movement is getting better at understanding how to affect change in individuals and in communities. There are still challenges and obstacles to overcome but schools have the opportunity to lead the way and influence the next generation. The next step is to get your school prepared for the changes ahead.

The tools

With an awareness of the contexts surrounding sustainable schools, it's time to look at the practical tools for creating an Eco-School. There are four key tools that you can use to prepare yourself for the journey. The tools allow you to justify your

"TOOLS OF THE TRADE"

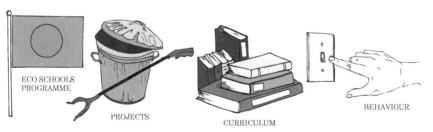

The Tools of the trade: Eco Schools programme, Projects, Curriculum, Behaviour

actions through the curriculum, provide a structure to your work, be creative and motivate pupils and adults to practise sustainable behaviours. These are introduced in this chapter and developed further on in this book.

Tool 1: curriculum

The first tool for school environmental management at your disposal is the curriculum. Although sustainability is currently included in the curriculum, science, citizenship, enterprise, geography, language, maths and information technology can all be taught through the context of environmental management and the topic is easily linked to curriculum goals across all stages. It provides opportunities to measure, problem-solve and communicate with others and can, of course, help to foster positive attitudes towards sustainability. It is also a very practical context for learning – a real thing to do – thus complementing modern-day theories on how children learn through experiential and meaningful activity.

As a professional teacher you will be skilled in linking topics to the curriculum, but many of the resources and lesson plans available highlight which area of the curriculum can be addressed. The Eco-Schools Scotland website (http://www.ecoschoolsscotland.org/page.asp?pg=118) contains very useful curriculum maps showing topics and their curriculum links.

Tool 2: the Eco-Schools programme

The next tool in your armoury is the international Eco-Schools programme – www.eco-schools.org.uk. This initiative is a ready-made environmental management programme for schools. It is a practical tool to involve pupils in environmental management and it will help you to structure your actions and provide guidance in how to set up and run an environmental management system (EMS). Get to know the programme well so that your efforts will result in a Green Flag award. The programme requires you to fulfil the elements of an EMS and channel activities through various topics such as Litter, Waste, Energy, Transport, Water, Biodiversity, and Health. Not all the topics need to be covered to get an award, but the whole school must be involved at some stage and work must be pupil-led. If your school is not already registered, visit your country's Eco-School website. Read about the programme and get the basic elements together. The programme is about having a structure in the school that allows for eco-projects to be carried out effectively; therefore you will need to structure your efforts as follows:

- Form an Eco-Team (committee).

- Carry out an environmental review.
- Create an action plan.
- Monitor and evaluate all your projects and systems.
- Link work to the curriculum.
- Involve the wider community.
- Have an eco-policy.

It is essential that this structure incorporating all the above points is in place in order to achieve Green Flag status although it is often neglected by many eager schools. The section later in this chapter entitled Environmental management basics carries more about this programme and environmental management in general, while Part 2 of this book outlines projects that have planning and monitoring at their heart to help you comply with the requirements of the programme.

Tool 3: awareness of behaviour

Be aware of some of the behavioural barriers to sustainable change in your school and in the community. By first identifying the non-sustainable behaviours in your school you can then investigate why these occur. Through observing or by inter-viewing people, you can build a picture of the problem and then work out the solution. For example, pupils might not be reusing paper, but interviewing them about this might reveal that they think it's best to recycle it. A simple solution might then be to do a lesson on reusing and providing paper-reuse trays in each classroom. The section entitled Encouraging sustainable behaviour change, later on in this chapter, shows you how to encourage good habits through a behaviour change methodology.

As an Eco-Teacher you are tasked with changing people's behaviours by motivating and persuading them. Awareness of what motivates children and adults will stand you in good stead when presenting new eco-projects. Primary school pupils can be encouraged in different ways, but first of all be aware that pupils' sustainable behaviour is often motivated by a need to help 'save the planet'. To maximise this enthusiasm, get them thinking about the 'big' issues such as the threat to polar bears or the impact on people of rising sea levels. Link climate change to stories about animals and people to conjure feelings of empathy and a need to help, and be aware that personal stories and pictures are more effective at engaging people than just facts and figures.

Secondly, children often see the practical measures, such as recycling paper, as a fun activity; but encourage them further through competitions and rewards, perhaps giving a trophy to the best recycling class of the week. Stickers and praise also go a long way to supporting their feelings of being an environmentally friendly person.

Adults, too, are aware of the big environmental picture and also engage with the more human side of climate change and the thought of the environmental legacy being left to their children and grandchildren. Use this as a way to inspire and motivate them. Also, adults are often motivated to take action for reasons that are perhaps more personal and closely related to them, such as increasing domestic fuel bills, which can encourage them to reduce their own personal energy use.

Research has shown that people respond when they are given a great deal of praise for their green behaviours and so encourage the use of heroic images and language when engaging with people. The use of superheroes works a treat and can help inspire children in particular.

Tool 4: projects

The fourth tool is the project work itself, designed to reduce each pupil's footprint in three key eco-topics:

- litter
- waste
- energy

There are many projects set out in *Part 2* of this book but these should be preceded by one fundamental project – a footprinting exercise.

Footprinting is taking a measurement of the school's impact on the environment. Such a project can vary in scope; for example, some measurements only look at carbon consumption while others may include wider factors such as the carbon involved in the staff commute. This can become complicated but there are several tools available to use, a good list of which can be found at http://greenschools.net/article.php?id=271; however, one of the best was developed in Scotland and found at: http://www.educationscotland.gov.uk/schoolsglobalfootprint.

A calculation tool allows you to measure the elements of a footprint, such as energy use and waste generation. In order to calculate your school's footprint you will have to take measurements through activities such as recording energy readings and carrying out a waste audit. Make sure you know which figures you have to collect and then, once you have them, you can input them to the calculator.

Using the curriculum, the Eco-Schools programme, the awareness of behaviour change and fun and effective projects will lead to the fulfilment of your eco-objectives. In order to use these tools appropriately, read through the chapters in this book and begin to build your Eco-School.

Environmental management basics

Chapter 1 outlines the need for sustainable schools and one way to achieve these is through applying the principles and practice of environmental management to school eco-work. As an Eco-Teacher it is, therefore, useful to be aware of this discipline.

Environmental management is a method for ensuring that an organisation uses the fewest natural resources possible. It can be broadly defined as 'a decision-making process that regulates the impact of human activities on the environment'[7] and it can significantly reduce waste and harmful impacts, which is fundamental to the principle of sustainability. It has become ever more important as the realisation of climate change impacts is felt across the world.

Environmental management and schools

Environmental management is, in general, a broad field; but, as it applies to schools it means making decisions as to the most practical measures to adopt the most sustainable procedures. A school impacts upon the environment with three of the key impacts being the litter it produces, the waste it generates and the energy it consumes. There are important reasons for managing these impacts. With litter, schools must ensure that they avoid littering the local environment; otherwise they could be fined up to £2,500 plus a daily fine until the litter is cleared. When it comes to waste, the local authority must dispose of waste appropriately for health reasons and, because of pressure on landfill sites, the more waste a local authority produces the more landfill tax it must pay. The Carbon Reduction Commitment Scheme means that the participating local authorities are committed to reducing carbon, including that used in school buildings. Those that succeed in doing this are rewarded, but those that fail can be financially penalised. Environmental management practices can, therefore, help a school to plan, to take action and show how it complies with legal requirements and manage its resource use effectively and without incurring penalties.

How to implement environmental management

Incorporating environmental management into the working of the school is made easier by the Eco-Schools programme, an environmental management system (EMS) based on the principles of the discipline (found at www2.keep britaintidy.org/ecoschools). The fundamental steps in running an EMS are shown in Illustration overleaf where the Eco-Team is formed and then goes up the staircase one step at a time. It is generally this programme that schools use to tackle sustainability issues in a measured way and to structure and formulate eco-learning. An EMS, such as the Eco-Schools initiative, is usually a paper-based checklist of tasks to carry out founded on an initial environmental review, an action plan document and a robust system of measurement, usually kept together in a ring binder folder. The Eco-Schools programme guides you through the essentials of running an EMS, dividing action between sections headed:

- Environmental Review
- Environmental Policy and Eco-Code
- Meetings minutes
- Action Plan
- Litter, Waste and Energy

The folder forms an ongoing record of your work, showing clearly the plans, actions and impacts of your eco-work and this is a sound base for making sure your eco-efforts are legitimate.

Understanding how these principles and practices are applied can be looked at in three examples of school environmental management in action.

Example 1: prevention and measurement

Preventing harm is the obvious environmental goal and this means looking at the processes that lead to eco-damage. Environmental managers investigate how something like litter is impacting on the local community and consider ways to reduce that impact by asking questions and finding answers. For example, one line of enquiry might be, 'How does litter from the school end up in the street outside?' An investigation or review takes place and it is discovered that the litter-bins are overflowing after lunchtime. Solutions are then drawn up and acted upon as part of an action plan – in this case more bins are installed in

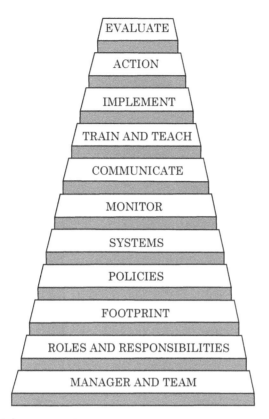

Key environmental management steps

the playground. Throughout this process, measuring takes place in the form of counting the number of pieces of litter in an area as quantitative evidence before the new bins are installed and then followed up with the same type of evidence after the new bins are in place.

Example 2: measuring and training

A different investigation might ask, 'How can the school reduce the amount of waste it generates?' A waste audit might be carried out at which point it is discovered that paper is being put into normal waste instead of the recycling bins. The solution and action is for the Eco-Team to talk to the whole school at the next whole-school gathering and remind everyone to put paper in the recycling bins. A follow-up waste audit then provides evidence of the impact of the action. In this example the measuring and the teaching of the new behaviour were key to the goal.

Measurement and record keeping

Example 3: record keeping and monitoring

Keeping records is an important element of environmental management and is best seen in practice through energy monitoring. Good practice would see the Eco-Team start by recording meter readings and keeping regular records. An action plan is drawn up, and it is decided to have a team of light monitors go round switching off lights at break and at lunchtime. The regular recording of the electricity meter readings shows the impact this new system has.

These examples show school environmental management in practice and to get these actions underway you, as the Eco-Teacher, need to get organised by understanding your role, the key tasks and what you might need to help you.

Key tasks of an Eco-Teacher

The profile of the person most suited to the job of Eco-Teacher might read as someone who is:

- Passionate about environmental issues.
- Able to connect with children.

- Familiar with the curriculum and understands the place of eco-work within it.

- Able to dedicate one or two hours every week.

- Familiar with the Eco-Schools programme.

- Willing to develop a professional approach to environmental management through attending training courses, reading and researching.

- Prepared to handle a budget for eco-improvements and has the authority to take decisions or influence those that do.

If you meet most of these requirements you are well on your way to being an expert Eco-Teacher, but perhaps there are some areas you need to develop or need help with. Being passionate is certainly fundamental, because this enthusiasm for the subject can be spread to the other Eco-Team members and on through the whole school. Other requirements for the job can be developed, but most important is: knowing what the job entails, being given time to do it and having the school management on board; certainly when it comes to budget decisions. See *Case study 3 – Environmental management: putting theory into practice*, as an example of a teacher that has gone through this process.

Typically, this person has no formal environmental background or training which is why this book exists: to help provide theory and understanding for those in this responsible role. Typical tasks for you as an Eco-Teacher are to:

- Form and meet with a school Eco-Team as regularly as possible.

- Carry out an environmental review.

- Plan and action environmental improvements.

- Measure, monitor and record resource use and keep records updated and current.

- Implement an EMS such as the Eco-Schools programme and work towards gaining Green Flag level.

- Encourage staff, the whole school and the local community to get involved in projects and give talks and training where necessary.

- Work closely with local authority and other environmental groups that provide assistance and expertise.

To help you achieve these tasks you will first need to form a team consisting of pupils, staff and the local community. You then need time to meet this group and to carry out the tasks you agree to do. Depending on the size of the school, there may be a lot to do so try to dedicate as much time as possible for coordinating tasks. You will benefit from expert advice so make sure to contact the local authority environmental department or community groups. Working closely with the local authority and supporting groups and people such as energy managers, waste education officers and Eco-Schools officers allows you to take advantage of expertise and to learn from those that have environmental management backgrounds. These people, however, are not always experts in working with children and cannot be in the school all the time so it is up to you, as the school's Eco-Teacher, to carry out the regular tasks and provide the projects and materials that will make eco-work fun, effective and focused.

You will also need a budget, so agree with management that you can put some money towards essential tools such as litter-pickers, high-visibility jackets, clipboards, measuring devices, recycling bins, etc.

Create your folder of work, sectioning it as mentioned earlier and review the actions that have been taken. Use this book to help you find ideas and plan and implement the projects in *Part 2*. The first task is to undertake an Environmental Review by completing a questionnaire, (see the example in *Appendix 2* or a version available on the Eco-Schools website, http://www2.keepbritaintidy.org/ecoschools/gettingstarted/environmentalreview). This questionnaire allows you to review the school's resource management and helps identify where you may need to take action to reduce environmental impact. As part of the initial review, you can footprint the school and record the findings. In *Part 2* of this book, a litter review, waste audit and energy audit activity are all recommended and these provide a method for capturing a snapshot of where the school is in terms of its resource consumption. The resource provided by http://www.carbonpartners.org.uk is an excellent way to input your findings and discover what the school's footprint is and even compare it with other schools. Another useful document is the School's Global Footprint found at http://educationscotland.gov.uk, that offers activities to teach how the school uses up natural resources. A third option is Think Leadership's 'Green Audit' resource at http://www.thinkleadership.org.uk/audit.cfm. All the actions you identify can be put into an order consistent with the approaches in the section called Routes to sustainability in Chapter 1, as this can help structure your plan of attack and help put your actions in a relevant and balanced order.

Environmental projects should be planned carefully, but often school eco-projects are too ambitious and so they fail. Therefore, try to keep goals and objectives realistic. Do not expect to compost all of the school's fruit waste in one compost bin. Think about what is achievable. To help, follow a planning strategy called 'SMART' where project goals are **s**pecific, **m**easurable, **a**chievable, **r**ealistic and **t**imed. Here is an example:

Specific – detail what you are going to do. Don't just write 'reduce energy use' but rather quantify the action; for example, 'reduce by ten, the number of lights left on every lunchtime'.

Measurable – count how many lights there are.

Achievable – can lights be checked every lunchtime?

Realistic – is it reasonable to expect them to be switched off by everyone, every lunchtime?

Timed – when will it be completed?

These headings are designed to make sure you have thought through what it is you are going to do. When you have your specified objectives prepared the next step is to draw up an action plan. There will no doubt be lots of things you will or already have identified and there are plenty of activities to implement in *Part 2*. These projects and actions follow environmental management principles so that you don't need to plan all the steps yourself. Simply following the step-by-step actions will make sure you stick to good practice but do remember, however, to record all your activities including measurements and readings, as this information will show off your work to any eco assessors that come to visit your school.

Finally, it's time to write an eco-policy, a simple statement that shows all school users that the school is committed to its environmental obligations. This is a formal record indicating that you have reviewed resource use and are committed to reducing impacts. In schools, this policy is often made into a poem or rhyme.

The tasks of the Eco-Teacher are ongoing and projects happen daily, weekly and termly, in classrooms, playgrounds and the local community and among all the pupils in the school. The goal should be to continually strive for improvement and to reach Green Flag status as quickly as possible while maintaining robust systems that help to minimise the use of natural resources. Following the steps outlined in this chapter will help you implement and run your environmental management system. The more projects you carry out the more comfortable you will become with the processes required and the feeling of understanding the principles of running an eco-friendly school.

Routes to sustainability

The Department for Education (formally Department for Children, Schools and Families) recommends that a 2020 sustainable school is one that:

- Puts sustainable development at the heart of the school ethos and demonstrates it in management practice.
- Embeds sustainable development in teaching and promotes it in communities.
- Uses sustainable development to motivate pupils, enhances their enjoyment of learning and ultimately raises achievement and standards.
- Views the whole curriculum and extra-curricular activities as a means of providing an education for sustainable development, and uses approaches that enable pupils to develop knowledge, skills and values through experience.
- Develops leadership and management practices that promote the core themes of sustainable development.

These goals can be achieved by planning and doing and a useful tool, produced by the Department for Education entitled 'Planning a Sustainable School' can help you set a vision for your school and get you started. However, the practical actions in reducing your school's footprint are many and there are different ways, or routes, to achieve tangible improvements. For example, some Eco-Teams may decide to do all the 'easy' stuff first, like clearing litter from the playground, while a different strategy might be to focus on the biggest elements of the school's footprint, such as the heating of the school. Each strategy has its merits but they have drawbacks as well. Too much time concentrating on one topic, for example, can mean that more pressing environmental improvements are delayed, while jumping across topics can lead to a loss of focus and forgetting to address key issues.

A balanced approach, however, where projects blend ease, fun and effectiveness, is recommended. Carefully considering your strategy and structuring your approach means finding a balanced route that takes into account the different factors that keep the school moving towards sustainability in a meaningful way. Energy use has a much larger footprint than waste or litter and so you might ask whether it is best to start by addressing that topic. However, maybe you think the waste-related projects are more exciting and decide to do those. This chapter outlines different approaches to help you plan your own route and find a balance that suits you and your school.

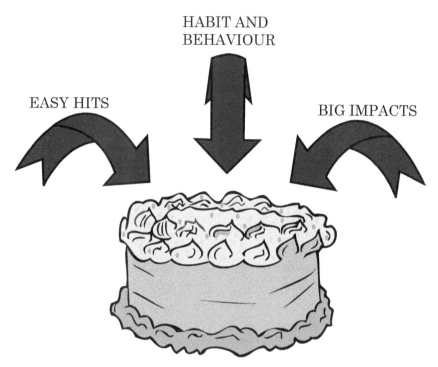

EASY HITS

HABIT AND
BEHAVIOUR

BIG IMPACTS

CAKE: The recipe for success

Part 2 of this book is arranged into three different topics: litter, waste and then energy, but this doesn't mean that covering the topics and their projects in this order is necessarily the best strategy for you.

'Easy-hits' approach

One approach is to tackle the 'easy hits' – those that can be implemented without much difficulty and realise quick results. The great advantage of this approach is that improvement is immediate and this can encourage people as they see progress being made.

An example of an easy hit is clearing litter; a project which can show an immediate, visual improvement and all that is required is a set of litter-pickers and some willing pupils. Easy! In the waste topic, introducing scrap-paper trays immediately lessens the amount of paper being used – just weigh the reused paper and post results to advertise the waste improvement made. Fitting low-energy bulbs in lamps quickly reduces energy consumption and all this takes is to go and buy the appropriate bulbs and screw them in where needed. The disadvantage of this strategy, however, is that spreading action across different topic areas means a loss of focus on a single topic.

Topic approach

The topic approach is about tackling one sustainability topic at a time, for example, litter. This strategy provides continuity, focus and depth to the learning. The topic can be followed along a linear approach as new projects and actions improve upon systems and help to embed behaviours and the actions maintain relevance while the topic is live. The advantage of this approach is that it is easily understood where the Eco-Team is concentrating its efforts; however, motivation and excitement may wane.

Big impacts approach

Addressing the larger elements of the school eco-footprint can realise savings in carbon and money and the benefit is that this approach can reduce the school's eco-footprint significantly. Heating can account for around 58% of a school's energy consumption[8] and far outweighs the impact of energy for other uses and, therefore, it may seem a logical place to begin an eco-campaign. While this is desirable it may not be the most exciting project for pupils, as much of the work to be done would involve the local education authority – fitting double-glazed windows for example. Also, progress may be slow.

Small-scale to large-scale approach

Eco-projects should eventually engage the whole school, but you may feel that you want to start small to ensure systems and techniques work before rolling them out to a wider audience. This is certainly good practice. Some schools allocate certain topics to certain year groups, where one class may be learning how to compost while another engages in energy use. The advantage in this is that lessons can be learned from how one class tackles the issue, such as learning how much organic waste the class produces, how quickly the compost bin gets filled and how it is best managed.

The whole school may be engaged in all the issues eventually but through different topics at different times.

Habits and behaviours approach

Changing habits and behaviours has the advantage of being a low-cost strategy.

Applying the principles of the '4 E' methodology, a planned system followed up by posters, classroom lessons and whole-school talks are the key ingredients to encouraging new behaviours in pupils and staff. (See the section: Encouraging sustainable behaviour change in Chapter 1 for a full explanation of the 4 E methodology.) This approach can be fun, engaging and straightforward

Table 2 Projects matrix

(ETA = Eco-Team action, CL = classroom lesson, WSC = whole-school campaign)

Easy hits	Topic	Big impacts	Small to large scale	Habits and behaviours
School litter pick (ETA/CL)	Litter	Playground litter prevention (ETA)	Class Litter-pick leading to whole-school campaign (CL/WSC)	The paper reuse collection scheme (ETA)
Tidy dining hall (ETA)	Waste	Organising a paper recycling collection (ETA)	Waste-free packed lunch (WSC)	Clear the plate (WSC)
Lost and found tray (WSC)	Energy	Compost food and garden waste (WSC)	Managing an indoor wormery (ETA/CL)	Staffroom campaign (ETA)
Energy loss foiled again (ETA)		Catering and suppliers packaging reduction (ETA)		Respect our resources campaign (WSC)
Tea-time tales (ETA)		Energy audit (WSC)		Switch on to switching off (WSC)
Power rangers (ETA)		Heat audit (ETA/CL)		
IT and energy efficiency (CL)		What's hot (ETA)		
		Light monitors (WSC)		

to implement. Campaigns to switch off lights, clear litter or recycle paper can be encouraged every couple of weeks, but bear in mind that habits and new systems take some time to bed in and that certain tools – like recycling bins, may be needed.

Table 2 sets out different projects to undertake according to which type of route you wish to take your school down. For example, if you want to show immediate impact then tackle the projects listed under 'Easy hits'. If you want to take a balanced approach then tackle projects from the different headed approaches.

Balanced approach (recommended)

The balanced approach suggests that motivational projects be intertwined with focused, high-impact projects while involving the whole school in several Eco-Schools topics. It is a blend of the different approaches over a period, perhaps a school year, which results in environmental improvement at the same time as creating a sense of fun around environmental management. Gradually campaigns begin to encourage new habits but while these are bedding in, the Eco-Team can itself work on projects that make the most significant carbon savings. The projects and campaigns will be fun and will inspire the pupils and staff to support the causes. This blending also keeps the Eco-Team motivated and the whole school encouraged. The change in focus on three different topics is interesting and ties in with the requirement for Eco-Schools Green Flag status. The initial projects can be kicked off in the first term and, as new systems become routine, new projects and campaigns can be introduced.

Throughout this approach, measure and document the impact of the actions; for example, count how much litter was collected, weigh the paper recycled and record gas and electricity usage. Show these results to the rest of the school to keep them motivated and to highlight where the school can further improve its environmental performance.

Table 3 Recommended, balanced approach

Action	Approach	Effect
Daily litter picks (litter)	Small scale – big campaign	Fun and motivating for pupils.
Whole-school litter-pick in playground (litter)	Easy hit	Stimulating and tangible results.
Paper recycling system (waste)	Big impact	The system will take time to bed in, but it involves pupils taking responsibility and will make a big difference to school waste.
Energy audit (energy)	Big impact	Requires investigation by the Eco-Team, but findings will help to gather evidence needed for improvement and can lead to significant carbon savings. No immediate tangible evidence of improvement but results are interesting.
Heat audit (energy)	Big impact	Because heating has such a significant impact this audit will contribute to a big impact. Mostly work for the Eco-Team.
Switch on to switching off campaign (energy)	Habits and behaviours	Keeps everyone involved with a fun whole-school project. Impact will be significant once the behaviours are routine.
Light monitors (energy)	Easy hit	Easy and tangible results. Follows on from switch off campaign.
Reduce food waste campaign (waste)	Habits and behaviours	Another fun whole- school project with long-term impacts.
Paper reuse trays (waste)	Habits and behaviours	Easy to implement in each class and should quickly become routine.
Compost campaign (waste)	Big impact	Reduces waste and great educational tool.

The *Action* part of this book is set out as litter, waste and energy to make it easier for you to correspond actions with the Eco-Schools programme topics. Working through one topic at a time is not the most efficient or effective approach, so to adopt a balanced approach use Table 3 and cross-refer to *Part 2* of this book. You can tick off the projects and actions as you go through them. When you launch your eco-programme, explain to the school that you will be working on the three topic areas.

Review the needs of your school and decide on your approach and which topics and projects might best fit your school. Sit down with the Eco-Team and make a clear plan. The reward will be a school making inroads into its footprint while making eco-education fun.

Encouraging sustainable behaviour change

When a new environmental system is implemented in a school it can take time for pupils and staff to adapt. For example, if the school decides to start composting then staff and pupils will be expected to put their fruit waste in the compost bin instead of the classroom rubbish bin. A new system like this requires people to change their previous routines and habits but this behavioural change can be difficult to achieve. Without considering how best to facilitate and prepare for these types of behavioural changes, the new system will be less effective.

Much research has gone into understanding how best to encourage people to adapt to new sustainable ways of living. Social psychologists have developed methodologies, often used by environmental planners when preparing to introduce new initiatives into a community, and one such approach – The 4 Es of sustainable behaviour change – can be easily used in school environmental management planning. The 4 Es are: **e**nable the action; **e**ngage people in the action; **e**xemplify the action; **e**ncourage the action.

The 4 Es: enable, engage, exemplify, encourage

Enable

Enabling sustainable action is providing people with the information, resources and authority to make that action possible. Without these, the desired action may not occur. Examples of enabling sustainable action in school are:

- Providing tools (such as litter-pickers, recycling bins, paper reuse trays or even technological solutions such as lights that switch off automatically).
- Providing information (such as how to switch a computer to sleep mode).
- Authorising time (such as for pupils to take meter-readings).

Engage

People can be engaged in sustainable action by raising their awareness and getting them interested and involved. It is important to engage everyone that is being asked to act, so that they are aware of what is being asked of them and they are able to adapt their behaviours accordingly. The key to effective engagement is using stimulating approaches to interest people in the action. Whichever method of engagement is adopted, it should be imaginative and memorable and involve the Eco-Pupils wherever possible. Forms of engagement in school include:

- Giving a presentation to staff.
- Giving an inspiring whole-school gathering talk to pupils.
- Sending informative letters to parents.
- Putting up colourful posters around the school.
- Handing out leaflets made by pupils.
- Creating songs, paintings, sculptures, dance which promote the action.

Exemplify

Exemplifying sustainable behaviour is showing others that this type of behaviour is normal. When people accept that there is a 'norm' then they are more likely to act in this way. Exemplifying is often forgotten about when planning a change, implementing and using an eco-noticeboard and and regular updates at whole-school gatherings are good ways to remind people of 'normal' green behaviours and standards. A school can exemplify sustainable behaviour through:

- Ensuring that the Eco-Team set an example that others can aspire to.
- Creating an environmental policy that everyone must adhere to, as this helps to establish a set of standards across the school.
- Emphasising that eco-action is taking place in other schools in order to reassure people that sustainable activity is normal.

Encourage

Encouraging people helps them to act by providing them with an incentive. Rewards or punishments can act as forms of encouragement but a positive approach is more often the most successful. Different people respond to different forms of encouragement but the most effective are:

- praise
- house points
- stickers
- certificates
- competitions
- charts and graphs showing success
- time out of class.

Classes that are underperforming environmentally can be encouraged to do better. Teachers and other school users also need to be encouraged, and approaches for them might include:

- Charts displaying school energy savings as a result of eco-work.
- Positive messages on the notice board thanking people for their efforts.
- Prizes to the most eco-friendly teachers of the term.
- Progress towards Eco-School status.
- Eco-days that motivate everyone.

Encouragement needs to be considered regularly, so successes must be communicated consistently and rewards kept fresh and relevant. Take a look at the illustration and see if you can spot how the 4 Es have been applied.

Can you spot the 4 Es in action?

Questions and answers regarding the 4 Es

The following are questions I am most frequently asked by teachers about using the 4 Es to encourage sustainable behaviour change and the answers I give. These will help you to understand how best to use the 4 E methodology as a tool in becoming an eco-school.

Q: *I sometimes find lights are left on despite reminding the pupils to switch off and putting up 'Remember to switch off' signs around the building. How do I make sure everyone switches off all the time?*

A: The most effective method is perhaps sending pupils around the school and switching-off lights at break and lunch-time. This exemplification can rub off on others. Rewards through competitions are also useful but these have to be kept fresh, exciting and relevant.

Generally speaking, non-sustainable behaviours can occur for several reasons:

- human characteristic
- habits
- attitudes
- lack of information
- lack of facilities.

Human characteristic – Forgetfulness is a normal human trait but it can lead to non-sustainable behaviour. A planned approach to minimising the likelihood of forgetfulness is required.

Habit – Old habits can be difficult to break and new habits difficult to form.

Attitude – Laziness is one type of negative attitude that can stop people walking across a room to switch off a light. This type of attitude creates thinking such as *Leaving one light on doesn't really matter* or *Someone else will switch off the light.* Attitudes such as these can be challenging to change.

Lack of information – For example, simply not knowing where a light switch is may prevent someone switching off that light. Likewise, if a school user is unaware that the school is trying to reduce its energy consumption, they may not be concerned about switching off lights.

Lack of facility – In some cases, non-sustainable human behaviour can be overcome by a facility such as technology. With lighting, passive infrared movement detectors can detect when there is no movement in a room and switch off the lights automatically, thus minimising human forgetfulness.

These barriers to sustainable behaviour can be overcome by adopting a methodology that takes these factors into account.

Q: *Are there case studies of schools that have used this approach?*

A: See *Case study 1 – The 4 Es in practice: introducing composting.* When a sustainable initiative succeeds it is often because each of the 4 Es has been applied. To maximise the potential for success, use the *4 E Planning Tool* in *Appendix 3*.

Awareness of these principles will aid the understanding of the rationale behind the actions listed in the *Action* section of the book and make the Eco-Teacher a better-informed and more effective environmental educator.

Q: *Most of the pupils act sustainably already, so why should I attempt something new?*

A: Most pupils acting sustainably all the time is excellent, but all pupils acting sustainably is even better! Training children to be sustainable now will help them develop their environmental attitudes and influence their behaviour choices when they are older.

Q: *Why is the 4 E sustainable behaviour model so important? I have already engaged the pupils at whole-school gathering and have put up signs and provided recycling bins. I always praise them when they act sustainably and I always exemplify good behaviour.*

A: Review each sustainable system in school and make sure this is the case. It may be that signs need updating so that they are noticed, incentives need to be refreshed to keep people motivated or that new technical innovations are available. Avoid complacency; regularly review practice and keep abreast of developments and best practice as many schools lose their Green Flags after resting on their laurels.

Q: *Isn't it normal to forget to switch off lights occasionally?*

A: The 4 Es approach aims to minimise the prospect of people forgetting to act sustainably.

Q: *What does Eco-Schools say about sustainable behaviour and the 4 Es?*

A: The Eco-Schools material suggests that behavioural change will occur if the elements of the programme are implemented but there is no mention of behavioural change methodology.

Q: *Can we still create a more sustainable school without following the 4 E model?*

A: Even without rigorously applying the 4 Es to every eco-initiative, sustainable behaviours can still occur; however, using the model makes those behaviours more likely. An environmental auditor will look for signs of sustainable behaviour and this will be evident from what rubbish is in the bins, what materials lie in recycling receptacles and if lights are found left on. Littering is one such behaviour that is easily identifiable and many schools have failed assessments because litter prevention was not embedded into their pupils' behaviour.

Q: *Is it time consuming to implement the 4 Es?*

A: The likelihood is that the school eco-initiatives already feature many of the principles of the 4 E model and perhaps a sign or a new form of encouragement is all that is required. Review or audit each practice to see if the system currently in place is effective. It may be that litter still occurs, that some recyclable material is placed in normal bins and that, occasionally, lights are left on. Compare the current system against the 4 E model by using the planning tool and identify any missing aspects of the model within the current system. Implement any measures that are required. The Eco-Pupils should be able to conduct much of this work, thus freeing teacher time.

Q: *Can sustainable behaviour be taught through the curriculum?*

A: The curriculum includes environmental education, citizenship and enterprise education, and there are many opportunities to engage pupils through the formal curriculum. Exemplifying positive sustainable behaviour should be an aspect of the Eco-Teacher's role, but other teachers in the school may have to be engaged through meetings or formal training sessions. Enabling and encouraging are more likely to feature in the environmental management role of the Eco-Teacher.

Q: *What are the sustainable practices an environmental auditor is looking for?*

A: The sustainable energy, waste and litter behaviours that a school's pupils and staff should display are listed at the beginning of this section.

Q: *In which order should the 4 Es be implemented and is one more important than the other?*

A: The method of approach depends upon each initiative and the current system in place. See the *Action* section of the book and follow the steps.

Q: *Once the 4 Es have been implemented will all the pupils behave sustainably all the time?*

A: The 4 Es approach increases the likelihood of sustainable behaviour occurring, but to maximise the chances of the pupils and teachers acting sustainably, consider what really motivates them and make incentives and rewards relevant and worth working towards. For pupils, time out of class, house or individual points, stickers or just pride in being the best class, can really motivate them. Competition is a very effective encouragement tool, whether it is class against class or even school against school.

Q: *Some staff and parents don't share the same enthusiasm for our eco-work. How can they be motivated?*

A: Some people are resistant to change, which can be due to a perception that new initiatives will take up their time or they have seen initiatives fail in the past. The financial cost of taking action might deter some business managers or perhaps they are simply not interested in environmental issues. Overcoming these barriers and changing perceptions can be difficult but school staff can be motivated in numerous ways such as:

- Rewards, praise and thanks, or even by the giving of cakes if targets are reached.
- School management enforcing eco-policy.
- Exemplification of sustainable behaviour by peers.
- Highlighting the benefits of change.
- Regular communication of eco-initiatives.

Q: *How does the school enable action if there are no facilities or there is limited finance available?*

A: The ability of people to behave sustainably can often be restricted by physical, financial or social barriers. Physical barriers might include that the fabric of the building is energy inefficient; a concrete playground restricts composting; light switches and sockets are difficult to reach. Examples of financial barriers might be that the school has no funds for eco-work or that it is in a socially deprived area. Social barriers could include that vandalism restricts the use of recycling or compost bins or parents don't support eco-initiatives.

Although there may be barriers, there are often solutions. The local authority, for example, may be planning to invest in upgrading school buildings; environmental organisations can often provide tools and expertise for sustainable initiatives; and, socially, more people are becoming aware of the need to care for the environment. Patience and persistence is one of the desirable requirements of anyone involved in initiating environmental change.

Q: *Can parents be influenced to help the school with its eco-initiatives?*

A: Parents can and should be engaged in sustainability. The school can play a leading role in developing sustainable attitudes in the community by, for example, urging parents to consider the environmental impact of the food and packaging their child brings to school. As children develop environmental attitudes through their schooling, they can help pass these attitudes on to their family members.

Schools can also involve parents in environmental projects wherever possible, and often parents and grandparents are able to assist with gardening or composting or other eco-work that needs to be done. Parents can be reminded that their attitudes and actions influence their children and, as the school is trying to develop positive environmental behaviours in its pupils, parents should support this aspect of schooling by behaving sustainably at home.

Q: *The school has many visiting specialists and substitute teachers. How can they be encouraged to behave sustainably in the school?*

A: If the school has adopted the 4 E model effectively, then visitors should find it easy to behave sustainably. To ensure that they do, create an information sheet to give any visitor environmental information, such as what the school recycles, where to find recycling bins, how to use the printer to print double-sided and so on.

A carefully planned approach to implementing sustainable systems is more likely to result in the appropriate behavioural response from pupils, staff and others.

End of chapter references

1 Sustainable Development Commission (2006), 'UK Schools Carbon Footprint Scoping Study'. London, p.15.

2, 3 The Met Office (n.d.), 'Climate change'. Available from: http://www.metoffice. gov.uk/climate-change/guide/how (Accessed 08/03/13).

4   UK, Department of Children, Schools and Families (2008), 'Brighter Futures, Greener Lives'. London, p.11.

5   The Carbon Trust (2007), 'Schools: Learning to improve energy efficiency'. CTV019, London, p.3

6   Eco-Schools (2013), 'Eco-School Stats', Eco-Schools. Available from: http://www.ecoschools.org.uk (Accessed 08/03/13).

7   Barrow, C.J. (2006), *Environmental Management for Sustainable Development* (2nd Edition). Abingdon: Routledge.

8   The Carbon Trust (2007), 'Schools: Learning to improve energy efficiency', CTV019, London, p.4.

2 Taking action on litter

Introduction to litter management

Litter can be defined as 'rubbish put in the wrong place' and in schools this means rubbish lying in the playground or in the immediate surrounding area, rather than stored in waste bins. This waste comes in the form of anything 'unnatural' and in schools it mainly consists of food leftovers, wrappers, cartons and crisp packets; and it is not just pupils who create litter but passers-by, traffic and local businesses too. The school is legally responsible, however, for minimising these occurrences and ensuring that they are doing all they can to remain litter-free. The consequences of schools creating litter include the financial implications of the authorities clearing it up and the potential for the litter to cause injury to young children and animals. Understanding litter management is extremely important for schools and failing to deal with litter appropriately is one of the most common reasons for schools being denied an Eco-Schools Green Flag.

Eco-Schools and litter

Schools working through the Eco-Schools programme will be aware that litter is the one topic that they must cover and, therefore, this is usually tackled first because of its importance and also because it is a relatively 'easy hit'. A good Eco-School litter management system is one that is robust and effective where the clearing of litter is conducted regularly. Addressing the topic should include:

- Daily clearing of litter from the playground.
- Frequent monitoring and evaluating of the litter at school and in the local area.
- Whole-school awareness of the litter policy and related campaigns.

See Table 4 for an example of what a litter management system and its processes might look like.

Table 4 Typical actions of a good school litter management system

Action	Description
Record figures	Record the total amount of one day's school litter
Photographs and evidence	Take photographic evidence before, during and after a litter-pick
Monitor and evaluate	Before starting any litter campaign, measure the amount of the material before starting your actions Have a rota showing who collects the school litter and where and when it is collected Record the number of people involved in your campaign
Involve the community where possible	Use parents and other adults at home to spread the environmental word

When an Eco-Schools assessment is carried out, the school must be litter-free on the day. If pupils are interviewed they should be able to explain what they have learned about the reasons for avoiding littering.

Know your litter

Before starting a litter management and education campaign it is useful to be aware of some of the background facts, such as the legal, social and environmental issues around litter.

Legal issue

Local authorities enforce litter legislation such as the Environmental Protection Act 1990, which makes state-funded schools responsible for ensuring that their grounds are kept litter-free by setting a 'Cleanliness Standard' of which there are four levels of cleanliness that the school must adhere to. These are:

Standard A – No litter or refuse.

Standard B – Predominantly free of litter or refuse apart from some small items.

Standard C – Widespread distribution of litter.

Standard D – Heavily littered with significant accumulations.

An area such as a road or park or school is given a ranking or 'zone', according to how intensively it is used by members of the public – either high, medium, low or special area; schools are classed as medium during term-time and low during holidays. Each zone has an allocated response time in which the litter needs to be cleared to 'A' standard. For medium intensity this is one day and, for low intensity, 14 days. Should this fail to happen then a fine can be imposed on the school of up to £2,500.

Nobody wants to see schools fail their litter obligations and so help is at hand through the local authority and other environmental agencies that can usually provide information and resources for schools' attempts to remain litter-free and avoid penalties. Contact your local environmental education officer or visit websites such as: http://keepbritaintidy.org or http://www.litteraction.org.uk/ for assistance.

Social issue

People's attitude to litter is often to blame for litter issues. Many people use a range of excuses for littering, often blaming the council or youths thinking that a small piece of litter won't do any harm but cumulatively, of course, it does.

There are four types of litterer, classed as:

- 'inconvenients' – too much trouble, someone else's problem
- 'ignorants' – unaware of the effect of littering
- 'wilful arrogants' – it's ok to litter, everyone else does it
- 'anti-establishments' – deliberate litterers.

These types of attitudes can be prevalent in the pupils' parents, but developing and fostering attitudes of non-litterers in children can reflect back to their families and help create a cleaner, more litter-free area around the school. This helps people feel safer and have more pride in their surroundings, as well as helping to reduce the financial costs of cleaning up.

People aren't always the cause of litter, however. Sometimes rubbish that has been placed in a bin can be blown out by the wind or even pulled out by birds, eager to get at food scraps. Foxes and other animals often rip open plastic and, when this happens, rubbish spills out and becomes litter.

Environmental issue

However litter occurs, it has negative environmental consequences, including harm to animals, marine life and birds. Carelessly discarded wrappings and containers can trap and suffocate wildlife, plastic bags can end up in the sea and be mistaken as food by fish, and cigarette butts can end up in water causing pollution. More background information on the impacts of litter can be found on the DEFRA, the RSPCA and the Marine Conservation Society websites; but children can be taught about these impacts through powerful images found in the information pack 'How To Conduct a Whole School Litter Campaign' produced by the Campaign for the Protection of Rural England (see the website www.cpre.org.uk).

Safety issue

When working with children and litter, the question of safety often arises and it is indeed extremely important that teachers and their pupils are aware of the risks and practicalities of clearing litter. Inside school grounds children should always use gloves or litter-pickers and, when outside of school, high-visibility vests are strongly recommended. A risk assessment of areas where community litter-picks might be conducted should also be completed, especially when near roads or rivers. Everyone taking part should be made aware of how to avoid handling hazardous waste such as drug-related litter and dog poo. Essentially, tell children to avoid touching it and call your local environmental health officer if areas have a high frequency of this type of waste. The *Litter-pick project* section in this book provides further advice on safety.

Did you know...?[1]

- Local authorities spent £885 million on street cleansing in 2009–10.
- 2.25 million pieces of litter are dropped in the UK every day.
- One in two people litter.
- Smoking-related litter is found at 81% of all sites surveyed in 2009–10 with fast food litter present on 24%.
- Between April 2008 and March 2009 over 30,000 fixed penalty notices were issued to people caught littering.
- Plastic litter will never rot away.

Taking action on litter

- The largest landfill in the world is in the Pacific Ocean where an area twice the size of Texas contains floating rubbish from across the Earth.
- There are four types of litter classification – dangerous, offensive, unhygienic, environmentally incompatible.
- One million sea birds die every year from ingesting or becoming entangled in marine debris – often from plastic bags blown into the sea.[2]

Resources for litter management

When addressing the litter topic there are certain pieces of equipment, materials and resources you will need.

Equipment

When out on litter-picks make sure you have appropriate equipment, such as high-visibility vests, gloves and litter-pickers. These can be purchased at http://www.litterpickersdirect.com/ or at http://www.helpinghand.co.uk. Waste bins are also vital tools in the fight against litter so check out http://www.amberol.co.uk or http://www.themebins.co.uk to buy fun and appropriate bins.

Classroom

For classroom materials the education pack called 'How to Run a Litter Campaign' produced by The Campaign to Protect Rural England (www.cpre.org.uk) includes background information, advice, powerful litter images and worksheets to support lessons. Supporting posters and stickers for any litter campaign can be provided at www.keepbritaintidy.org.uk. Further guidance is available through the useful litter knowledge-bank sheets found on the website.

Frequently asked questions

Q: *If we have litter in the playground, will we fail a Green Flag assessment?*
A: Yes. You must keep the grounds litter-free.

Q: *Who pays the fine if the school has littered?*
A: The school. The fine can be £2,500.

Understanding school litter management

School litter management is about four main things: analysing, clearing, reusing and reducing. There is a crossover between elements of litter management and waste management, where the reduce, reuse, recycle hierarchy applies, and there is also a reliance on the cooperation of parents and the wider community. Litter management involves a campaign teaching all school pupils about litter issues, planning fun and effective projects and taking action to reduce and clear litter from the school and the community. It starts by first looking at occurrences of litter and discovering why and how it came to be litter, rather than waste in a bin, and then taking action to prevent it arising in the future. This approach is complemented at the same time by a system of litter clearing, usually by groups of pupils on a regular basis. Once litter is collected, some of it can be reused – and some of it even made into artwork back at school. The ultimate goal is to reduce litter and waste at source, by preventing it from entering the school in the first place. This can be done through projects that are also relevant to reducing waste, such as the *Waste-free lunch* (see how to run this project in *Chapter 2*).

Alongside litter management practice, behaviour change techniques – using the 4 Es of engaging, enabling, exemplifying and encouraging – can be applied to make sure pupils and the local community know why and how to avoid creating litter and how to avoid litter. To achieve this, be prepared to teach how to analyse litter problems, devise action plans with the Eco-Team, undertake litter-picks across the whole community and measure the success of their litter projects. Remember to advertise successes and reward positive litter behaviours to make sure that good habits stick.

Special event litter-picks are those that take place outside the school grounds, usually in parks, on streets or on beaches. These events can be used to involve members of the wider community and can help pupils better understand the impact of dropping litter by letting them see the consequences for the environment at first hand. Such an event may be held once per term but, as with any school outing, the day must be carefully planned. Often, however, local environmental organisations and community groups run days for school groups and can help with planning.

When teaching litter issues, be aware that different types of litter need to be tackled in different ways, and so you should be clear about advice you give on dealing with drug-related litter, dog poo, gum, food and wrappings, and answers can be found as you read through this chapter.

Once you are clear on what projects you are going to do, meet up with the Eco-Team and get started. Beginning in the school grounds, tasks involve pupils in surveying school grounds, identifying 'hot-spots', recording evidence and using appropriate equipment, and then using the findings to report progress across the school. Follow the steps as set out in the projects listed later on.

Getting started with litter management

School litter management is a continuous process and so the actions listed in this section are to embed effective litter management into school life and integrate the curriculum at the same time. The starting point in a litter management project should always be the analysis of litter in the school grounds. The Eco-Teacher, Eco-Pupils and whole school are involved in the project.

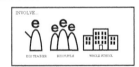

Take action

- School grounds analysis.

The findings from this project inform the litter clearing project that will follow, by showing pupils where to concentrate their litter-picking efforts.

Project 1: school grounds analysis

This project allows the school to see exactly what type of litter problem it has by looking in detail at where it collects. Pupils get to use practical skills in identifying and problem-solving while also having fun being outside. The project also provides a snapshot of the litter in school against which future litter analysis can be compared.

- **Action 1. Eco-Team:** meet to discuss the project.

  Gather the Eco-Team and explain that they will be analysing the litter in the school playground by recording what they see. Explain that the findings will be used to draw up a rota and instructions for the clearing of litter in the playground. Points to discuss are:

  - When the analysis will take place – after break or lunch is a good time.
  - The idea of 'hot-spots' where litter can collect.
  - How to record evidence – photographs and counting pieces of litter.

- **Action 2. Eco-Team:** gather resources.

  Once the plan has been drawn up, gather together pencils, a sheet of paper to record evidence and a camera.

- **Action 3. Eco-Team**: conduct analysis.

  Walk around the playground and find areas where litter has collected. Write down where these areas are or mark them on a map of the playground. Ask the pupils to try and count or estimate the number of pieces of litter in each area. Take photographic evidence.

- **Action 4 Eco-Team:** analyse findings.

  Back in school analyse the findings by adding together the number of pieces of litter that were found. Look at the photographs and agree where the litter 'hot-spots' are. Ask why the Eco-Team think these areas have more litter than other areas. Explain to pupils that this is where litter clearing efforts will be concentrated.

- **Action 5. Eco-Pupils:** present findings to whole school.

  During a whole-school gathering get the Eco-Pupils to present their findings and introduce the concept of a whole-school litter-pick and what this means in a positive sense to everyone who uses the school.

- **Action 6. Eco-Pupils:** update eco-noticeboard.

  Have the pupils show their evidence on the eco-noticeboard.

Now that you have a good picture of the school's litter situation you can begin planning the solution for a litter-free school. The next project is setting up and running a whole-school litter-pick so that all pupils are engaged in the act of clearing their litter. Following on from this, the Eco-Team will assume responsibility for organising regular litter clearing.

Litter clearing

Litter clearing may not sound the most glamorous eco-project but it can give you a relatively quick win-win in terms of addressing environmental harm. It involves: drawing up a school-ground litter clearing rota; making sure there are appropriate tools to carry out the tasks; measuring and monitoring the amount of litter collected and displaying and reporting evidence of the team's litter clearing efforts.

Through litter clearing projects the pupils learn and practise skills in planning, measurement and reporting. The litter-pickers themselves experience the feeling of responsible citizenship and greater self-esteem through being part of a positive environmental project.

There are two key projects in school litter clearing that you can do that take place in the school grounds, in the local community and in the classroom.

Take action

- School litter clearing system
- Shrinking crisp packet supporting classroom lesson (see *Appendix 4*)
- Community litter-pick
- Litter art supporting classroom lesson.

Pupils from across the school can be involved, because the act of picking litter is straightforward. Safety is the biggest issue so always make sure children know how to stay safe. Also, remember to measure and record how much litter is being collected, because this will provide evidence when you begin your campaign to reduce litter coming into the school.

Remember to make sure you have enough litter-pickers, gloves and, if outside the school, high-visibility vests to ensure all pupils involved are safe.

Frequently asked questions

Q: *Is there anywhere we should not pick litter?*
A: Be aware of the dangers of roads, rivers and beaches; no litter pick is worth injury or harm to a child.

Q: *How much do tools cost?*
A: Prices vary for things like litter-pickers and high-visibility jackets. Eco-Schools sell litter packs for around £25.

Q: *Are there any organisations that can help with community litter-picks?*
A: Ask your local council or look up local community groups. Another school might even be able to lend you some of their tools and equipment.

Q: *What should I do if a child touches hazardous waste?*
A: Always carry wipes and a First Aid kit when out on such trips, in case a child touches dog-poo or other unpleasant and dangerous substances. The telephone number of a local doctor is also useful. Avoid areas where there may be drug-related litter. If you are going to a park, 'sweep' the area before to ensure there aren't any needles lying around. Everyone involved should be wearing gloves. However, if a needle does pierce, seek immediate medical advice.

Q: *What is the best way to measure the amount of litter collected?*
A: Take measurement tools such as spring balances and hang collected bags of rubbish from them. Small bags, rather than large, are easier to weigh.

Q: *What type of litter is useful for reuse?*
A: Metal cans, glass and plastic bottles are recyclable. Have separate bags for such waste but make sure they are empty. Crisp packets and wrappers can be used in art displays.

Project 1: organising a school litter clearing system

A system of regular litter clearing from the school grounds, initiated by the Eco-Team, will prevent the build-up of litter. The responsibility is then spread across the whole school with other classes taking turns at clearing.

- **Action 1. Eco-Teacher:** engage peers.

  Explain to other teachers and staff that the Eco-Team is going to initiate a system which will mean the school is cleared of litter on a daily basis. Explain that the Eco-Team will initiate the project and draw up a rota so other pupils across the school will be involved.

- **Action 2. Eco-Team:** meet to discuss the litter-picking system.

  Remind the group of the findings from the school grounds analysis. Discuss how a litter-picking system functions, pointing out the need for a rota. Decide when the best time is, for example: perhaps towards the end of lunch break.

- **Action 3. Eco-Team:** instruct on the potential dangers of litter and litter picking.

  Before going to the school grounds, talk to pupils about hygiene and emphasise that tools must be used and gloves worn. Remind everyone to wash hands after the activity.

- **Action 4. Eco-Team:** gather resources and tools.

  You will need gloves and/or litter-pickers, plus bags to collect the waste, including separate bags for any recyclable waste. Take spring balances or other measurement tools and writing and recording materials (paper, pencils, camera).

Checklists are a useful tool

- **Action 5. Eco-Pupils:** collect litter.

  Head for the hot-spots previously identified. If the grounds are extensive, decide where you might find litter. The whole school area need not be cleared every day.

- **Action 6. Eco-Team:** measure.

  Once the litter has been collected, weigh the amount. Record the total.

- **Action 7. Eco-Team:** engage and encourage peers by reporting results.

  Post the results on the eco-noticeboard, so that others can see litter is being cleared. Celebrate when less litter is collected. Consider reporting results at the whole-school gathering.

- **Action 8. Eco-Pupils:** review the system.

  Have a meeting to discuss how the litter-pick went. Was there anything that could be improved upon for next time? Were there enough tools; did you have enough time, etc.? Record the answers and apply any learning for the next day's litter pick.

- **Action 9. Eco-Teacher:** consult with colleagues and agree a rota.

  Once the Eco-Team has trialled the system, agree with teachers that all pupils will have a turn at litter clearing and schedule in each class for a week at a time.

- **Action 10. Eco-Teacher:** instruct all litter-pickers how to pick litter safely.

  The Eco-Team can instruct others in how to pick the litter. This could be done in a short training session on the new litter-pickers' first day.

- **Action 11. Eco-Team:** post rota across the school.

  Place the rota on all notice boards so everyone knows when it's their turn.

- **Action 12. Whole school:** celebrate and reward.

  Celebrate the collection of litter and give a reward to those individuals or classes who have done particularly well. Keep this system in place to ensure it becomes embedded into school culture.

- **Action 13. Eco-Teacher:** enable classroom teachers to teach the *shrinking crisp packet* lesson (see *Appendix 4*).

  Provide classroom teachers with the *shrinking crisp packet* lesson plan.

Supporting classroom lesson: shrinking crisp packet

This lesson uses litter found on litter-picks to make art that can support the litter campaign. See the lesson plan in *Appendix 4*.

Project 2: community litter-pick

Community litter-picks can be great fun because the impact is immediate, visible and tangible; they take place away from the school, which makes it exciting for everyone; and they involve pupils and adults working together. The Eco-Team can carry out a community litter-pick; however, it is more effective and more usual for a class to go on an excursion such as this. Willing parents and/or other volunteers with a vested interest in keeping the community litter-free often join pupils and staff on the pick. This helps forge school–community links, which is an aspect of the Eco-Schools programme. You may first wish to contact the local council environment team to see if such an event, such as a 'community action week', is already being planned. However, if nothing is in the pipeline, take some time to plan it yourself.

When organising your own event, your plan should follow the key steps that are:

- Risk-assess the area.
- Borrow or buy the resources you'll need.
- Invite parents and others in the community to help.
- Plan the event, keeping it to a reasonable length to avoid people getting bored.

Think how you will manage the activity on the day, paying attention to what you will do with the litter you collect. Remember to measure and evidence your efforts. Also, remember to separate items that can be used in school for *litter art* lesson.

- **Action 1. Eco-Teacher:** seek assistance.

  Find out if there are any community litter-picks being planned by checking with the local council or other organisations.

- **Action 2. Eco-Teacher:** read instructions from Keep Britain Tidy.

  Keep Britain Tidy has published a very useful document called 'Litter – Organising a Clear Up', fully explaining how to conduct a community litter-pick. This can be found on the Keep Britain Tidy website by accessing archived material at th following address:

  http://www2.keepbritaintidy.org/Expertise/Research/KnowledgeBanks/Default.aspx

- **Action 3. Eco-Team:** identify a hot-spot and risk-assess.

  Go out with the Eco-Pupils and find an area that will be suitable for a litter-pick. Carry out a risk assessment.

- **Action 4. Eco-Team:** meet the Eco-Team to discuss planning.

  Discuss how to carry out the event. Points to discuss are:

  - How to invite people to the event.
  - How the litter will be collected.
  - How the collected litter will be measured.
  - How reusable litter for the *litter art* lesson will be kept separate.
  - How to remain safe when clearing litter.

- **Action 5. Eco-Team:** involve a class.

  Invite a class to the event, considering which age group might be most appropriate.

- **Action 6. Eco-Team:** invite parents and the wider community.

  Send invites to parents and advertise for helpers in the wider community, perhaps through posters in local shops.

- **Action 7. Eco-Team:** gather resources.

  Gather litter-pickers, high-visibility vests, thick gloves, spring balances and rubbish bags. Contact the council or other organisations to borrow equipment or alternatively buy what is needed at www.helpinghand.co.uk.

- **Action 8. Eco-Team and class:** conduct the litter-pick.

  When everything is planned, conduct the litter-pick, remembering to record your efforts. Photograph the litter collected and weigh it, taking note of all the measurements. Separate reusable litter ('clean' packets, bottles, cans, etc.) to use in the *litter art* lesson. Remember to thank all the participants.

- **Action 9. Eco-Team and class:** analyse the findings.

  Back at school discuss the experience and what was found. Have the children draw conclusions about the value of keeping the community clean. With the weight of the litter collected, calculate how much litter could be dropped over a year.

- **Action 10. Eco-Team and class representatives:** report to the whole school and the community.

  Make a presentation to give to the whole school showing the litter-pick in action and reporting how much litter was collected. Also, give feedback to the community, highlighting the impact of the litter-pick and asking for everyone's help to keep the area as litter-free as possible.

Supporting classroom lesson: litter art

With the collected litter brought back to school, the classroom teacher can teach the *litter art* lesson. See the lesson plan in *Appendix 5*.

Reducing litter

When something like a plastic bag is binned, it can still end up as litter – often when it has fallen from an overflowing rubbish bin or been blown from the landfill site on which it was dumped. So, when it comes to preventing litter, reducing it at source to avoid these problems is the most effective approach.

The school grounds analysis should have revealed what types of litter were found in the playground, so you can begin to investigate how it got there and who might have been responsible for it. It is then time to play detective and begin projects that take place in three physical areas – the school grounds, at home and in local shops. It is likely that the litter found will have been produced at source in these places with packets, wrappers, plastic bags, cigarette butts and marketing material the most likely types of litter found. Within these lines of investigation, the Eco-Team and other pupils will engage with children, parents and the wider local community, educating and encouraging them to reduce the sources of litter in and around the school. This set of projects includes opportunities to fulfil community engagement responsibilities and can also be tied in with waste reducing projects that have similar goals.

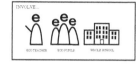

Take action

- Leave litter indoors and litter and wildlife supporting classroom lesson
- Stop the drop
- Befriend a bag
- Make a newspaper bag supporting classroom lesson.

These projects and lessons require the application of skills in communicating with others. The Eco-Pupils will be asked to speak to their peers and teachers to create a system where packaging waste (plastic, cardboard, etc.), is disposed of as close to its 'end of life' as possible. Pupils will also engage with parents to discuss how to go about preventing unwanted mail becoming litter, while shoppers and shopkeepers will be the subjects of a project designed to promote the use of reusable bags and reduce the number of plastic carrier bags wasted.

Speaking to others requires a certain confidence and knowledge in the topic of discussion, so be prepared to make sure pupils understand why prevention is better than cure and discuss landfill sites and how litter can arise even after it has been binned.

Remember

When discussing litter reduction, the opportunity to discuss health and choosing healthy snacks over crisps and sweets is obvious. Point out that waste from apples and pears can be composted and so are better for people and the planet!

Birds can also be the source of playground litter if they are able to access waste bins. Often seagulls are able to pull out bags from bins, so try to have bins that have lids that are kept closed. Preferably, waste should be kept indoors as the first project suggests, taking the seagull menace out of the litter equation.

Frequently asked questions

Q: *What types of things can become litter?*
A: Anything, but lighter material, such as paper and plastic wrappers, has the potential to be carried by the wind and is, therefore, more likely to end up as 'waste in the wrong place'.

Q: *What types of litter can be reduced?*
A: Unwanted mail, plastic carrier bags and wrappers are easily dealt with by engaging people and pupils.

Q: *Litter means jobs for street cleaners, doesn't it?*
A: Street cleansing costs money that could be spent on other things. Preventing litter campaigns also create jobs.

Q: *What is the difference between waste and litter?*
A: Litter is described as 'waste in the wrong place'. Waste is when the use of a material has not been fully maximised.

Q: *Where can I get bins with lids ?*
A: The websites http://www.amberol.co.uk or http://www.themebins.co.uk provide suitable bins.

Q: *How can we get the community interested in litter prevention?*
A: Engage with people at home and on the streets. Ask people to pledge to help reduce litter and give them 'heroic' status for helping the campaign.

Q: *Does litter prevention have a big impact on the environment? Surely once waste is binned then the problem is solved.*
A: Even waste placed in a rubbish receptacle or recycling box has the potential to 'leak' out. Light material can be blown from bins, landfill sites or be scattered by birds and animals.

Q: *Are plastic bags a big litter problem?*
A: Plastic bags can end up in the sea where they are mistaken as food by marine life. Even biodegradable plastic bags still need to be managed properly as they will not automatically biodegrade in a landfill site where they are starved of oxygen and, therefore, unable to biodegrade.

Project 1: leave litter indoors

This project aims to encourage binning litter indoors, rather than in playground bins, and so reduces the potential for it blowing away or being accessible to birds and other animals. The binning litter indoors behaviour can be achieved by creating a system where snacks are either eaten before going into the playground or are opened inside the school and the wrapping binned before going outside. The system requires time set aside for eating snacks inside and/or litter monitors to 'police' doors to the playground checking that litter is being kept from the school grounds.

- **Action 1. Eco-Teacher:** teach litter prevention.

  Begin the project by gathering the Eco-Pupils and teaching them about the next step in litter management: litter prevention. Start by reviewing the school grounds analysis to see what types of litter were found in the playground. Discuss who might have been responsible for it being there and elicit that it might be pupils. Explain that the project will prevent wrappers, packets and other materials from getting into the playground and, therefore, reduce the chance of it becoming litter.

- **Action 2. Eco-Team:** plan a system.

  A system is required which will reduce waste material getting into the school grounds by stopping it as close to its 'end of life' as possible. Plan to provide a system that allows all pupils to place waste in rubbish bags before going into the school grounds. You may decide to have children eat snacks indoors or to have the Eco-Team hold open rubbish bags at the entrance to the school grounds.

- **Action 3. Eco-Team:** inform others.

  Before implementing the system, explain it to staff and to the whole school.

- **Action 4. Eco-Team:** draw up a rota.

  Draw up a rota of who is to stand by the doors collecting the waste. Begin with the Eco-Pupils but prepare to roll out the responsibility to other classes.

- **Action 5. Eco-Team:** gather materials.

  Gather rubbish bags, measuring devices, paper and pencils to be able to collect, measure and record the amount of waste collected.

- **Action 6. Eco-Team:** implement the plan.

  A few minutes before break-time, have the Eco-Team station themselves at doors accessing the school grounds. Have them collect any waste material from the pupils before they take it into the playground.

- **Action 7. Eco-Team:** measure impact.

  Once the waste has been collected then it can be weighed. The measurement should be recorded, so that it can be reported back to the rest of the school and be used as evidence in the eco-folder.

- **Action 8. Eco-Team:** report back and celebrate.

  Have the Eco-Pupils report back their measurement during a whole-school gathering. This is also an opportunity to thank everyone for taking part and to encourage pupils to continue using the system.

- **Action 9. Eco-Team:** place measurements on the eco-noticeboard.

  Share the results via the eco-noticeboard as a figure or with photographs or as a graph.

- **Action 10. Whole school:** share duties around the school.

  As the system becomes embedded and everyone knows how it works, share the responsibility around the whole of the school, so that other pupils are also involved.

Supporting classroom lesson: litter and wildlife

See the resource 'How to Run a School Litter Campaign', provided by the Campaign to Protect Rural England and The Wiltshire Wildlife Trust (www.cpre.org.uk). The story and images can be used in classrooms to support the litter prevention campaign.

Project 2: stop the drop

This project connects school with home by engaging pupils and parents in a common source of potential litter – unwanted mail. Unwanted mail, sometimes referred to as 'junk' mail, consists of flyers and letters sent by companies wishing to promote their products and services or it can be promotional and local 'newspapers' that exist mainly to advertise. It is, more often than not, put straight in the bin, but even then it still has the potential to end up being blown away on its journey from the waste bin to landfill site or even the recycling centre. Again, tackling the source of the material is the best solution and in this case it can be relatively straightforward. Solutions include asking parents of pupils to place signs on their doors asking that no promotional material be put through their letterbox.

The second element to this project is to encourage people to sign up to the Mail Preference System that can reduce unwanted mail being sent. Pupils will be involved in communicating and persuading, and the impact can be measured in the difference in weight of unwanted mail received in households before and after the campaign and also in measuring the number of people in the community that got involved.

- **Action 1. Eco-Team:** discuss and plan the campaign.

  Begin the project by looking through the actions that need to be carried out. Discuss and agree who will do what and when. Agree the aims and measurement process.

- **Action 2. Eco-Team:** prepare materials needed.

  Copy the letter to parents explaining the objectives of the project using the template in *Appendix 6*. This will inform parents about the purpose of the campaign as well as asking them to register with the Mail Preference System.

- **Action 3. Eco-Pupils:** make letterbox signs.

  Signs should be made for each household, reading: *No promotional mail please. We are trying to reduce waste. Thank you.* Pupils can design these.

- **Action 4. Eco-Pupils:** whole-school talk.

  The Eco-Pupils should give a talk to all school pupils saying why unwanted mail is a problem. Explain that the project is in two parts: first to collect one week's worth of unwanted mail received at home and weigh it, reporting the amount back to the Eco-Team. Then, at the end of the week, householders should place the signs on their letterboxes and register with the Mail Preference System. Pupils take home the letter and the sign.

- **Action 5. Eco-Team:** measure the number people that get involved.

  Collect in the evidence from households and review it. Record the findings using the weight and the number of people that participated as evidence.

- **Action 6. Eco-Team:** repeat collection.

    Repeat the process one month later. By then, those parents that placed the signs on their letterboxes and/or registered with MPS should have noticed a reduction in the amount of unwanted mail they have received. The Eco-Team can weigh the new amount collected and, using the same calculation as before, work out how much unwanted mail has been reduced in the community.

- **Action 7. Eco-Team:** report, thank and celebrate.

    Report the results of the campaign back to the whole school via the eco-noticeboard and at a whole-school gathering. Communicate this back to the whole-school community, thank them for participating and celebrate the success by recording it as another step towards being a real Eco-School.

Project 3: befriend a bag

Around ten billion plastic bags are used in the UK every year[3] so reducing the use of these items can help prevent litter and waste. This project, therefore, is two-fold: first, aiming to promote the use of 'bags for life' (robust shopping bags which can be used in place of the plastic carrier bag) and, secondly, to encourage people to think about a second use for a plastic carrier bag as a bin liner as we usually have to put our rubbish into some form of plastic bag anyway.

The *befriend a bag* project involves school pupils engaging with shopkeepers and shoppers and encouraging them to adopt these behaviours. The project runs along the lines of planning how to engage shoppers and then going out and doing it. The number of people engaged is the measurement of success.

- **Action 1. Eco-Team:** plan who, when and where.

    The Eco-Team, and maybe children from other classes, should meet to establish the purpose of the project – to encourage people to reduce plastic bag litter through using a 'bag for life' and/or by reusing plastic bags as bin liners. Agree which local shops might be involved in the campaign and decide which pupils will speak to the shopkeeper.

- **Action 2. Eco-Pupils:** make signs.

    Make signs that promote 'bags for life' that could be placed in a shop window.

- **Action 3. Eco-Team:** meet local shopkeepers.

    Pupils, accompanied by an adult, can visit local shops and ask them to join the campaign. Ask if they will place one of the signs in their shop window and also if they wouldn't mind if shoppers were engaged outside their shop.

- **Action 4. Eco-Team:** engage shoppers.

    Engage shoppers by asking them two questions:

    1 Do you use a bag for life?

    2 Do you reuse plastic carrier bags as rubbish bags?

    They can provide their name as evidence of a pledge. Ask if they don't mind their name being placed on a *thank you* wall inside the school.

- **Action 5. Eco-Pupils:** record the pledges.

    Back at school, count the number of people that pledged. Record the evidence in the eco-folder.

- **Action 6. Eco-Pupils:** report, thank and celebrate.

    Put the names of those that pledged onto a poster or wall with a big 'thank you' and share this with the rest of the school and the local community.

Supporting classroom lesson: make a newspaper bag

A great practical lesson supporting the topic is making a bag from newspaper. A reusable bag can be made simply by folding and gluing old newspapers.

See the the website http://www.viddler.com/explore/ronansprake/videos/3/ for an example of how to make a bag from newspaper.

End of chapter references

1 Keep Britain Tidy (n.d.), 'Litter' Keep Britain Tidy. Available from: http://www.keepbritaintidy.org/KeyIssues/Litter/Default.aspx (Accessed 08/03/13).

2 Sea Turtle Foundation (n.d.), 'Marine Debris' Sea Turtle Foundation. Available from: http://seaturtlefoundation.org/marine-debris/ (Accessed 08/03/13).

3 We Are What We Do (2011), 'I'm Not A Plastic Bag' We Are What We Do. Available from: http://wearewhatwedo.org/portfolio/im-not-a-plastic-bag/ (Accessed 08/03/13).

3 Taking action on waste

Introduction to waste management

Reduce, reuse, recycle is the mantra that the school staff, pupils and local community should be familiar with if the school is to lower the amount of waste it sends to landfill. To do this, you will have to run a series of projects and actions that blend implementing systems and routines with fun, educational activities.

Waste, or rubbish as some call it, can also be referred to as an unexploited resource. Most material can be used again, which makes more sense than throwing it in a large hole in the ground. Although waste is not the largest element of a school's ecological footprint, needlessly binning material does not make environmental or economical sense. Landfill sites are smelly and dangerous as they produce methane, a greenhouse gas that is 23 times stronger than carbon dioxide. These sites are quickly filling up too and, to avoid contributing to these problems, schools should look at measures to reduce the waste they produce. The 2008 WRAP report 'The Nature and Scale of Waste Produced in Schools in England' showed that school waste amounted to 186,500 tonnes a year. Of this, food waste accounted for 46% of school waste, while 30% was paper and card, with 9% attributed to plastics. Paper recycling has certainly improved in schools in recent years, but there still exists opportunities to reduce, reuse and recycle all types of school waste as the report also revealed that only 13% of primary school waste is recycled. There are plenty of actions that you and the pupils can take to minimise waste and improve the school's recycling rate.

Eco-Schools and waste minimisation

Most schools working through the Eco-Schools programme address the 'Waste Minimisation' section early on, because many of the waste reducing actions are easy to implement. School waste management is assessed on the three key points that are:

- Monitoring and evaluation of waste levels.
- Whole-school awareness of and involvement in reducing waste.
- Robust waste management systems.

Monitoring and evaluation are essential when undertaking any Eco-Schools topic, not just waste minimisation. To meet the requirements of the programme, evidencing how much waste is being reduced, reused or recycled is crucial, because otherwise there is no quantitative proof of how much the school is diverting from landfill. It is good to record this type of data by weight, noting figures such as the weekly weight of the recycling bins as solid evidence of the school's waste minimising efforts.

With a whole-school approach necessary, all pupils and staff in the school should know the meaning of *reduce, reuse, and recycle*. Posters, recycling bins and reuse trays around the school building should enable everyone to take part in some form of waste minimisation. Recycling figures placed on the eco-noticeboard should also keep everyone informed of how the school is progressing. The typical actions of a school waste management system are set out in Table 5.

Table 5 Typical actions of a good waste minimisation system

Action	Description
Record figures	Record the total amount of one day's school waste through a waste audit
Photograph	Take photographic evidence before, during and after a waste audit
Monitor and evaluate	Before starting a waste campaign, measure the weight of the material before starting to reduce, reuse or recycle
	Regularly record the weight of recycling bins, reuse trays and material reduced
	Monitor the number of people involved in your campaign
Involve the community where possible	Use parents and other adults at home to get extra points for spreading the environmental word

The steps involved in implementing these actions are set out in the next section, but a good starting point for any waste project is to conduct a whole-school waste audit.

Know your waste

When delivering waste education it is important for you to be aware of waste issues and to build an understanding of the waste hierarchy: reduce, reuse, recycle. These and other terms surrounding the subject are explained below.

Waste: The disposal of a material, whether it has been used to its fullest potential or not.
Waste hierarchy: The order of waste disposal methods.

Waste hierarchy

Waste prevention: The preventing of waste arising in the first place. This is the *reduce* part of the hierarchy.

The 3 Rs – *reduce, reuse, recycle*

Reduce: To have less waste and to prevent it arising in the first place.

At the top of this hierarchy, and the most effective approach to preventing waste, is to *reduce* it, often referred to as *waste prevention* and, indeed, total UK waste generation decreased by 11% between 2004 and 2008.[1] Reducing waste in school has a crossover with preventing litter as both aim to avoid materials entering the waste stream.

Reuse: The reuse of a material without it changing form.

After a material has been manufactured it should be used to its full potential, and there are many school materials and objects that can be reused either for the same use or for a different purpose.

Recycle: The reprocessing of an already used material to make it into something new.

In the waste hierarchy, recycling is the next best waste management option after landfilling, but while there are many benefits to recycling there is still an environmental impact from the industry because of the energy used in collecting, bulking and reprocessing materials.

The recycling industry relies on there being a market for recycled products and so environmental educators should be aware of the need to teach their audiences to buy recycled goods whenever possible.

Incineration and energy from waste

Incinerating waste can create pollution; however, one potential benefit is that the gas can be captured and used as an energy source. There are several of these 'methane capture' landfill sites across the UK.

Did you know...?

- In 2005 around 72% of UK school waste was sent to landfill. [2]
- On average 45kg of waste is generated each year by every pupil in primary schools in England.[3]
- Landfill sites are filling up and it is estimated that parts of the country will run out of space to store waste by the year 2020.
- In a landfill site degradable waste produces methane – a very strong greenhouse gas 23 times more powerful than carbon dioxide.
- In landfill a banana can take two years to biodegrade; in a compost bin it takes only eight weeks.
- Landfill sites can be breeding grounds for vermin.
- Materials can take a long time to degrade:

- a paper bag – 1 month
- a rubber sole of a boot – 50–80 years
- a tin can – 80–100 years
- an aluminum can – 200–500 years
- Plastic 6-pack rings – 450 years
- Plastic jug – 1 million years
- Glass bottle – never.

Some wacky waste facts[4]

- Every year UK households throw away the equivalent of 3½ million double-decker buses (almost 30 million tonnes), a queue of which would stretch from London to Sydney (Australia) and back.
- On average, each person in the UK throws away seven times their body weight (about 500kg) in rubbish every year.
- In 2001 UK households produced the equivalent weight of 245 jumbo jets per week in packaging waste.
- Babies' nappies make up about 2% of the average household rubbish. This is equivalent to the weight of nearly 70,000 double-decker buses every year. If lined up front to end, the buses would stretch from London to Edinburgh.

Recyclable materials

Most of the contents of a school bin are recyclable. The types of material that are most commonly found in schools are:

- paper
- card/cardboard
- cartons
- plastic bottles
- metal
- fabric
- mobile phones
- compostable material.

Recycling collections for other materials, such as low-grade plastic used for sandwich wrappers, may be difficult to arrange because the cost of the collection may be uneconomic or the material is not in demand. Contamination by, for example, foodstuffs, can affect the quality of recycling material and is a potential barrier to recycling. Your local recycling company can give you information on what can be recycled, but for general information on recycling visit http://www.recyclenow.com.

Waste bin

Resources for waste management

When addressing the waste topic there are several good materials and resources you will need.

Equipment

When carrying out a waste audit you can often borrow from waste education organisations, such as the local authority; but, basically, you will need strong rubber gloves, spring balances, scales, recycling bins which can be bought at http://themebins.co.uk, and for recycled materials look up http://remarkable.co.uk.

Classroom

A waste audit instruction manual is useful, such as the excellent resource called 'The Standardised Waste Audit' found the Scottish Environment Protection Agency website on www.sepa.org.uk by searching 'standardised waste audit' or a good set of instructions exist on http://www.greenschoolsireland.org while http://wastebuster.co.uk is full of waste measurement lesson plans and activities for Key Stage 1 and Key Stage 2.

Frequently asked questions

Q: *Who should collect the recycling bins from around the school?*
A: The Eco-Team can set up the system, but responsibility should eventually be shared across the whole school.

Q: *Where should the recycling bins be placed?*
A: As close to the point of behaviour as possible. Have big signs around the school to direct people to the recycling points.

Q: *What happens to waste when you put it in a normal bin?*
A: Residual waste is usually taken to a local landfill site.

Q: *I've heard that recycling can get shipped to China. Is that true?*
A: Yes. Cardboard, paper and other material is a resource that is bought and sold across the world.

Understanding the school waste management process

There can be a lot of work involved in addressing school waste management, but often, usually out of sheer enthusiasm, the school takes on too much too quickly without clear planning or robust systems being put in place. The actions listed in this section, however, allow you to set up and follow waste management practice and integrate the curriculum in the process with tasks allocated among the Eco-Teacher, Eco-Pupils and classroom teachers.

This section of the book is organised according to the waste material that is to be reduced, reused or recycled, starting with paper, then food, then packaging. In each case there are guidelines on how to minimise that waste.

The school's waste management systems should be effective and the Eco-Team should ensure that the systems run smoothly with bins collected and emptied regularly and with the correct type of material going into each recycling bin.

Getting started with waste management

A waste audit offers the opportunity for you to analyse the school's rubbish and is a great learning opportunity for pupils. It also provides a baseline figure of the current waste situation in school against which future audits can be compared. The findings from a waste audit can aid the school's quest for a Green Flag.

Take action

A waste audit is a fundamental project which helps you see how much waste the school actually produces in a day. This can be a fun way to establish a baseline figure to calculate the waste footprint of the school.

INVOLVE...
ECO TEACHER   ECO PUPILS   WHOLE SCHOOL

- The school waste audit.

Project 1: the school waste audit

Plan to collect one day's total school waste. Collect it, measure the weight and the type of material found and record figures. The whole school and community can be involved.

- **Action 1. Eco-Teacher:** seek assistance.

  As waste audits can be a big undertaking, identify people that can help. The local council waste department or nearest environmental organisation may have carried these out before, so contact the recycling or waste officer.

  If there is no agency to assist and you feel confident enough to undertake the audit alone, then use the 'Standardised Waste Audit' guidelines.

- **Action 2. Eco-Teacher:** read how to conduct a school waste audit.

  Read the online instructions and prepare to collect, measure and record the total amount of school waste from one day.

- **Action 3. Eco-Team:** meet to discuss planning.

  Meet together to discuss how to collect one day's school waste. Points to discuss are:

  - How to do a 'walk-round' of the school recording where all the bins are and who will collect them for the audit.
  - How to collect waste at the end of a typical school day.
  - How to know which rooms or areas the rubbish bags came from.
  - How to store them overnight and ensure they are not thrown away.

- **Action 4. Eco-Teacher:** involve cleaning and caretaking staff.

  Explain the nature of the waste audit to cleaning and caretaking staff and ask for their assistance in ensuring that waste bags are collected and not thrown away.

- **Action 5. Eco-Teacher:** book a room.

  The best place for a waste audit is in a hall or large room, preferably well ventilated!

- **Action 6. Eco-Teacher:** inform and invite parents.

  Have an Eco-Pupil write a letter informing and inviting parents to the audit.

- **Action 7. Eco-Team:** collect and store the waste bags.

  The Eco-Team should collect and store the waste bags.

- **Action 8. Eco-Team:** conduct the audit.

  Conduct the audit the following day. Empty, sort and then weigh each of the materials. Record the weight of each. Remember to make sure that pupils are wearing gloves when handling waste.

- **Action 9. Eco-Teacher:** analyse findings.

  Meet the Eco-Pupils to discuss the findings and create an action plan for material that you are going to recycle.

- **Action 10. Eco-Teacher:** research the disposal options.

  Identify one material you are going to tackle and research the disposal options by looking for recycling companies, environmental organisations or the local council that can help you. Recycling is usually a good place to start in order to work up the waste hierarchy towards reusing and reducing.

- **Action 11. Eco-Team:** report to whole school.

  Present the findings of the audit to the whole school at whole-school gathering time or on the eco-noticeboard.

  The actions involved in reducing, reusing and recycling paper, food and packaging waste are set out in the pages that follow. Paper is one of the largest waste streams in school so it is a good material to start to reduce, reuse and recycle.

Paper

Paper in schools comes in many forms, including worksheets, jotters, art resources, junk mail and paper towels, so there are many opportunities to minimise wastage of this valuable material, from implementing paper recycling systems to adopting 'one paper towel only' policies. The actions involved in preventing paper waste are set out in this section.

Recycling paper

Most schools now have paper recycling collections in place but that doesn't mean that everyone always remembers to put their paper in the recycling bin. To encourage a better recycling rate the most effective paper recycling systems often display the following features:

- A paper recycling bin/bag/box in every class and office.
- Posters on walls to remind people to recycle paper.
- Collections of the paper by the Eco-Team, which are then placed in the playground recycling bin.
- The weighing of paper and the recording of results.
- Results posted on the eco-noticeboard.
- A good knowledge of how to recycle paper – with everyone 'in the picture'.

To avoid complacency and to ensure that the paper recycling system runs smoothly in the school, implement the relevant Paper Recycling Actions listed in the 'Organising a paper recycling collection' project.

Remember

Confidential papers can be recycled using a secure collection service, which may be offered by the recycling collection company.

Frequently asked questions

Q: *Can I recycle envelopes in paper bins?*
A: This depends on the collection advice. Glue and the plastic windows can reduce the quality of the recycled paper. Ask for advice from the collection company.

Q: *Can sugar paper be recycled?*
A: Yes, providing there is no glue or paint on it.

Q: *Can painted or glued paper be recycled?*
A: No. The glue and paint reduce the quality of the recycled paper so companies prefer not to collect this.

Q: *How do I know if something is paper or card?*
A: If it rips, it is paper. If it tears, leaving thicker fibres at the edge, then it is card.

Q: *Can paper towels be recycled?*
A: No. This is low quality paper usually at the end of its life. Added to that, the dampness makes this not worth recycling. Unused towels can be composted, however.

Take action

- Organising a paper recycling collection
- Making recycled paper supporting lesson plan.

Recycling figures should be shared with the school community and the results celebrated. These figures can be used as excellent evidence of monitoring and evaluation procedures. To keep the recycling momentum going, pupils can be encouraged through offering rewards for the 'Best Class of Paper Recyclers'.

Keep measurements logged in the eco-folder to show that the school is evaluating its performance and displaying good environmental practice.

Project 1: organising a paper recycling collection

Most schools already recycle paper and do it very well. However, pupils move on and the members of the Eco Team change so there is always an opportunity to review the system the school has in place and the following project helps ensure you have a robust system in place and that the pupils enjoy taking responsibility for the task.

- **Action 1. Eco-Teacher:** arrange a paper recycling collection.

  Contact the local council. It is likely that the school will get this service from their local council without charge.

- **Action 2. Eco-Teacher:** canvas school staff.

  Canvas the school staff for their opinions on how best the paper recycling system could be implemented in school. Involving staff will give them some ownership of the project and enjoyment celebrating the success of it.

- **Action 3. Eco-Teacher:** select classes to trial the recycling system.

  It is good practice to trial any recycling system before implementing it across the whole school. Select the class or classes you wish to trial the system in and inform their teachers.

- **Action 4. Eco-Teacher:** instruct Eco-Pupils how to run the paper recycling system.

  Competent Eco-Pupils can run the paper recycling system. Explain to the group that they will be collecting the paper from the recycling container in the trial class. The group must collect the container, weigh the contents, record the data and empty the paper into the big recycling bin.

- **Action 5. Eco-Pupils:** draw up a collection rota.

  The pupils should agree among themselves who is going to collect the recycling container and when. They can draw up a schedule with their names allocated to different days or weeks.

- **Action 6. Eco-Team:** engage peers.

  The Eco-Pupils should visit the trial classroom and explain to the class what they should put in the paper recycling bins. They can leave one copy of the collection schedule with the class teacher.

- **Action 7. Eco-Teacher:** review the trial.

  After a week of trialling the collection, review the system with the Eco-Pupils and agree any necessary amendments that need to be made.

- **Action 8. Eco-Team:** create 'The Eco-Pupil Recycling Company'.

  To create a successful recycling collection, the Eco-Pupils can set up their own recycling collection 'company'. They can create a company name, make paper recycling posters and a collection schedule showing who will collect the paper and when it will be collected, as this will be useful for their 'customers' – the class teachers – to know.

- **Action 9. Eco-Teacher:** roll out whole-school paper recycling.

  Now roll out the recycling system across the whole school by giving each class and office area a recycling bin. Engage the whole school by explaining the paper recycling system at a whole-school gathering.

- **Action 10. Eco-Team:** introduce 'The Eco-Pupil Recycling Company'.

  The Eco-Pupils can introduce their service to the whole school during a whole-school gathering and begin to visit classrooms to collect the paper, according to their rota.

- **Action 11. Eco-Pupils:** weigh and record results.

  Pupils weigh the collected paper, record the results on a graph and then place the paper in the recycling container.

  These actions should ensure an effective recycling system, but more understanding of paper recycling can be gained through supporting classroom lessons.

- **Action 12. Eco-Teacher:** classroom lesson.

  Provide colleagues with a copy of the *making recycled paper* lesson plan.

Supporting classroom lesson: making recycled paper

Each class teacher can teach the lesson on making recycled paper. See the lesson plan in *Appendix 7*.

Reusing paper

Once the paper recycling system has been established, the school can turn its attention to reusing paper. Paper reuse behaviour differs from recycling behaviour because now people are being taught to avoid putting paper in the recycling bin which, to some, may be confusing and seem contrary to what they were taught before.

Reuse allows a material to be used to its fullest potential such as writing on both sides of a piece of paper, filling up space in jotters, using newspapers and cards during art and reusing old envelopes to send internal mail.

Remember

Even with a paper reuse scheme in operation, people may still put paper in the recycling bin not realising that it had potential for reuse. Periodical audits of the recycling bins are a useful way of monitoring the success of the paper reuse scheme.

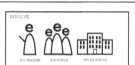

Take action

- Paper audit
- Paper raid supporting classroom lesson
- Paper reuse tray scheme
- Envelope reuse
- Newspaper
- Christmas card reuse campaign
- Card gift box supporting classroom lesson.

Keep measurements logged in the eco-folder to show that the school is evaluating its performance and displaying good environmental practice.

Project 1: paper audit

The paper audit lesson raises awareness of how much paper can be reused and provides a baseline figure to compare future paper reuse weights against. The activity is practical and hands-on and a good model of active environmental citizenship.

- **Action 1. Eco-Teacher:** Teach Eco-Pupils paper reuse.

  Teach the Eco-Pupils that reusing paper is better than recycling because it has less of an environmental impact. Instruct the pupils that they will be responsible for carrying out an audit in order to find out how much of the paper in the recycling bins could have been reused.

- **Action 2. Eco-Pupils:** collect paper.

  Pupils retrieve the paper recycling bins from around the school and take them to a central point.

- **Action 3. Eco-Team:** sort and find reusable paper.

  The bins should be emptied onto the floor so that all the paper is easy to rummage through. Get the pupils to look through the paper and put aside good quality, A4 office paper that has only been used on one side.

- **Action 4. Eco-Team:** weigh paper and record figures.

  The pupils should weigh the amount of reusable paper they have found. Keep the results in the school eco-folder where this will act as evidence for Eco-Schools assessors.

  Now that the Eco-Pupils understand there is a need to raise paper reuse awareness, a system can be introduced into each classroom. Trialling this in one or two classrooms for a few days is the best way to see if the system will work before introducing it across the whole school.

- **Action 5. Eco-Teacher:** enable teachers to teach the *paper raid* lesson. Provide colleagues with a copy of the *paper raid* lesson plan.

Supporting classroom lesson: paper raid

Each class teacher can teach this lesson teaching how to turn used paper into notepads and drawing books. See the lesson plan in *Appendix 8*.

Project 2: paper reuse tray scheme

The introduction of a paper reuse tray scheme follows the same pattern as that of the paper recycling system. Trialling the scheme in one or two classes before launching it across the whole school allows for any issues to be identified and resolved, making it more likely to succeed.

- **Action 1. Eco-Teacher:** source reuse trays.

  Source a tray or box, at least A4 size, for each classroom. Old shoeboxes, cardboard boxes or even cereal packets are suitable (and promote reuse). Pupils can decorate these later.

- **Action 2. Eco-Team:** introduce paper reuse to a few classrooms.

  Instruct the Eco-Pupils that they are going to introduce paper reuse trays to two or three classrooms. They should explain to each class that:

  - Reusing paper is better than recycling because less carbon is used to reuse than to recycle.
  - Reusing means making the most use of things before they are put in a bin.
  - From now on, if a piece of paper is used once, it can be placed in the class paper reuse tray.
  - The class should use the paper from the tray for drawings or rough working.
  - The Eco-Pupils will be coming around to check that paper is being reused before being recycled.
  - There will be an award (stickers/house points/class points/extra play) for the 'best paper reuse class'.

- **Action 3. Eco-Pupils:** give class talks.

  Pupils visit each class, giving their talk and leaving the paper reuse tray in the classroom.

- **Action 4. Eco-Pupils:** give staff talks.

  Pupils visit the school office to explain that the whole school is learning to reuse paper. The pupils should leave a tray with the school secretary, business manager and head teacher.

- **Action 5. Eco-Pupils:** review the scheme and extend it across the whole school.

  After a week of trialling the paper reuse tray scheme in a few classrooms, review its success, making sure that pupils are putting the correct type of paper in the reuse tray. Once the system is running well, extend it to every classroom in the school.

- **Action 6. Eco-Pupils:** weigh reused paper.

  Weigh the amount of paper collected in reuse trays for one week. Record the amount and note it on the eco-noticeboard as a way of encouraging everyone in the school.

Project 3: envelope reuse

Schools receive a lot of mail and the envelopes it comes in can be reused either as scrap paper or for reuse as an envelope again.

- **Action 1. Eco-Teacher:** engage staff in the envelope reuse tray system.

  Engage the teaching and administrative staff in the paper reuse campaign by asking them to reuse envelopes. Enable the action by supplying a tray or box where appropriate. Explain that envelopes that are in a good condition after being opened should be placed in the tray.

- **Action 2. Eco-Teacher:** supply address labels.

  Address labels can be bought at http://www.treesforlife.org.uk/products/ envelope_reuse_labels.php. Give a supply of these to each staff member and ask them to use these with old envelopes when sending a letter out from the school.

- **Action 3. Eco-Pupils:** weigh and record.

  As an additional piece of evidence for Eco-Schools, the envelopes collected can be weighed regularly and the figure recorded.

Project 4: newspaper

Newspaper is sometimes used to protect desks during art activities, but many schools prefer plastic sheets because they are durable and lessen the need to source newspaper. If there are newspapers in the school, they can be used for papier mâché or as a form of protective packaging.

- **Action 1. Eco-Team:** collect old newspapers.

  Ask people to bring in old newspapers from home so that there is a supply for art lessons.

Project 5: Christmas card reuse campaign

Around one billion Christmas cards are sent in the UK each year.[5] If, in a class of 30 pupils, each sends a card to their fellow pupil, then 900 cards have been sent. Multiply this across the whole school and you can see that there is potential to create a lot of waste.

The Eco-Team can make a difference by running a Christmas card reuse campaign involving the whole school and the community. Cards are collected and then made into gift boxes by the pupils.

- **Action 1. Eco-Teacher:** collect cards.

   Ask pupils across the school to bring in old, unwanted Christmas cards from home. The best time to tell everyone to do this is before the winter holiday break and again after the holiday, so that cards will not already have been thrown away.

   One card per pupil in the school will allow everyone the opportunity to make a box. Any extra cards that are collected can be kept to repeat the activity or be recycled. The type of card that should be used is plain, A5 size and without any additional decorations (ribbons, glitter, etc.) as these can make the gift boxes more difficult to make.

   Tell everyone about the campaign through a whole-school gathering or talks to each class.

- **Action 2. Eco-Pupils:** coordinate collection, measure and record.

   The Eco-Team can coordinate the drop-off point for cards. Once all the cards have been handed in, they can be measured and the total weight recorded. Keep this as evidence in the eco-folder.

- **Action 3. Eco-Teacher:** enable teachers to teach the *card gift box* lesson.

   Provide colleagues with a copy of the *card gift box* lesson plan.

Supporting classroom lesson: card gift box

Each classroom teacher can teach the lesson that promotes reuse through a fun way to make gift boxes by folding old gift cards. See the lesson plan in *Appendix 9*.

Reducing paper

Paper can be prevented from entering the school waste stream by limiting the need to use it through campaigns and policies and practices that include restricted paper towel use, printing and photocopying training, unwanted mail being stopped and using appropriately sized paper for letters. There are many good financial as well as environmental reasons to cut back on paper consumption, as the less paper that is used the less has to be bought. This section details how to implement these strategies.

Remember

Reducing waste can be challenging, but clear communication, encouragement and accurate measuring of waste-reducing practices will make reduction more likely.

Take action

INVOLVE...

ECO TEACHER   ECO PUPILS   WHOLE SCHOOL

- Paper towels
- Printing and photocopying
- Letters home
- Cards.

By implementing these projects the amount of paper in the school waste stream can be drastically reduced and the culture of sustainability enhanced.

Project 1: paper towels

Paper towels account for a large volume of overall school waste and they are preferred to cloth towels because of hygiene issues. It is unlikely that the school will be able to dispense with paper towels; but it can influence how many towels get used and thereby reduce overall paper towel waste.

- **Action 1. Eco-Team:** make a *One paper towel only* action plan.

  Discuss paper towel use. Inform the Eco-Pupils that they are going to promote the reduction of hand towel use. They will record the current amount of paper towel waste, give a talk to the school and make signs encouraging *One towel only*.

- **Action 2. Eco-Pupils:** audit paper towel waste.

  The team should identify areas of paper towel waste; most probably classrooms, toilets and the staffroom. They should then collect the bins in that area and record the weight of the towels in those bins at the end of one school day, keeping the evidence in the eco-folder. Remind pupils to wear gloves for extra safety when measuring paper towel waste.

- **Action 3. Eco-Pupils:** make signs.

  Make signs instructing people to use only one paper towel when drying their hands. Place these signs next to all paper towel dispensers including classrooms, toilets and the staffroom.

- **Action 4. Eco-Pupils:** infant paper towels.

  Visit infant classes and cut the paper towels in half, as smaller hands need fewer towels. They should tell the infants to use only one half towel when drying their hands.

- **Action 5. Eco-Pupils:** talk to each class.

  Visit other classes and explain the *One towel only* campaign.

- **Action 6. Eco-Pupils:** spot-check bins.

  Carry out spot checks by measuring the paper towel waste again a week after the class talks. Give out stickers to individuals/classes that are doing well.

- **Action 7. Eco-Pupils:** audit bins.

  Return to the bins measured previously and weigh the paper towels again. Record the results and compare them to the figures from before. By the end of this campaign paper towel use should have reduced.

Project 2: printing and photocopying

The school photocopier is a well-used machine. Unnecessary or erroneous copying and printing can lead to paper waste, not to mention wasted ink and electricity. To lessen this wastage, make sure that everyone using these machines knows how to use them.

- **Action 1. Eco-Pupils:** engage the staff.

  Place a sign by the photocopier asking people to copy carefully and avoid waste paper.

- **Action 2. Eco-Teacher:** enable effective photocopying and printing. Give staff the following tips:

  - Load classroom printers with 'scrap' paper.
  - Make one 'test' copy to make sure the copy looks good.
  - Copy double-sided when possible.
  - Print on scrap paper when appropriate.
  - Accidental copies can be put in the paper reuse tray placed next to the copier.
  - Give out instructions on the printing function on school computers.

- **Action 3. Eco-Teacher:** identify a print 'champion'.

  To ensure computers are set up to print effectively and that people know how to use the photocopier, identify a staff member that has a good knowledge of how to use the office machines. This person becomes the print champion and could be an office staff member or the IT specialist.

Project 3: letters home

Communication with parents throughout the year can result in a lot of paper being used, but schools are usually very efficient at keeping paper use to a minimum. The smaller the piece of paper the letter is written on the better, and using a 'siblings list' avoids two of the same letters going to one household.

Many people have access to email at home and using this form of communication is more environmentally friendly than paper letters, so implement a scheme that allows for more of this type of communication.

- **Action 1. Eco-Teacher:** discuss email communication.

  Meet management and the office staff to discuss the option of contacting parents for permission to send communication via email, explaining that the school is trying to help the environment by reducing its use of paper.

- **Action 2. Eco-Teacher:** issue a letter home.

  Get office staff to issue a letter to parents asking those who wish to be contacted by email to supply their email addresses.

- **Action 3. Eco-Teacher:** make an email list.

  With the office staff, make an email list and use this for corresponding with email parents.

Project 4: cards

The *Christmas card reuse campaign* and the *card gift box* lesson (from the last section) demonstrated what could be done with old cards, but it is preferable to reduce the amount being sent in the first place. This figure could be reduced by sending e-cards, having one big card for everyone to sign or finding another method of saying *Merry Christmas* such as a greeting ceremony.

Remember

Christmas card sending is a sensitive issue with some people, as they see the writing and sending of a card as an important part of Christmas celebration. If parents or children want to send lots of cards then let them.

- **Action 1. Eco-Teacher:** agree a card-sending policy.

  Meet school management to discuss reducing Christmas card waste. Suggest that the school asks pupils and parents to refrain from giving cards to everyone in their class and offer alternatives such as the *big Christmas card* (one per class or one for the whole school) or a *whole-school gathering Christmas greeting*.

- **Action 2. Eco-Team/Class pupils:** big card.

  The Eco-Team can make a giant Christmas card and decorate it or classroom pupils can make one for their own class.

- **Action 3. Eco-Team:** Organise a *Christmas whole-school gathering greeting*.

  Pupils can greet each other instead of sending a card. The greeting can be arranged at the end of a Christmas Holiday whole-school gathering. Organise the pupils in a way that allows them to greet their peers.

- **Action 4. Eco-Teacher:** staff agreement.

  If the whole school has agreed to reduce the number of Christmas cards being sent, ask staff to support the arrangement and reduce the number of cards they send.

Food

Food in English schools in 2008 accounted for around 46% of total school waste.[6] Of this amount, 25.3% was vegetables and 23.7% was fruit[7] which you can reduce by composting and through food-waste reduction campaigns.

Composting is a great way of minimising waste to landfill and is a critical element in reducing food waste. Compost itself is the soil-like substance created through the degrading of organic matter, which is collected in a bin or pile on top of soil or grass, turned occasionally and left to biodegrade. This degrading process attracts worms and other mini-creatures into the pile who eat through it leaving behind compost. The resultant product gives a substance ideal for growing plants and spreading on fields and lawns. Making good compost relies on getting a good balance between 'green' waste (for example, grass clippings and leaves), 'brown' waste (for example, fruit, vegetables, tea bags) and getting air into the pile.

Compost can also be made in wormeries that are like compost bins except that they are not connected to the soil or grass. This means that they can be kept indoors; ideal if there is no garden or suitable outside place for a compost bin.

The type of school waste likely to be composted includes:

- most fruit and vegetable peelings and cores
- tea bags
- coffee granules
- shredded paper
- card
- grass clippings
- leaves and twigs
- crushed eggshells.

Composting has many benefits for children, as they learn enterprising skills, are exposed to the outdoors and make an environmental difference all at the same time.

Remember

Some inner city schools do not have a soil or grassy area in which to place a compost bin. Putting a compost bin on top of concrete or even in a planter does not work because worms must enter the bin from the soil below.

School waste contains a lot of fruit and it can be tempting to place it all in the compost bin. Unless this type of material is matched by 'brown' waste, such as dry leaves, paper, or grass clippings, the fruit waste will make the contents too wet and, instead of compost being produced, a useless pile of sludge will form. Make sure this does not happen, as the sludge will need to be landfilled and, worse still, the school may be put off composting.

In rare circumstances vermin can be attracted to compost bins. Usually, this is because cooked food has been placed inside and the smell from this type of food waste can attract mice and rats. Avoid putting cooked food in a compost bin and place wire mesh under the bin if vermin problems are a concern.

Fruit peelings contain fruit fly eggs and, when the peelings are degrading, the flies hatch out. This can mean a few flies zooming out of the bin when the lid is lifted. If this becomes a problem, place a layer of cardboard on top of the compost heap.

Because of regulations regarding food waste, compost made at school should be used only within the confines of the school.

Frequently asked questions

Q: *Can cooked food be recycled?*
A: Not in a compost bin as the smell can sometimes attract vermin. Some types of closed composters do take cooked food, however.

Q: *What makes good compost?*
A: Get a balanced mix of 'dry' and 'wet' material, turn the compost occasionally and look after the bin.

Q: *Should I worry about vermin?*
A: A cooked food smell may attract vermin. Put wire mesh under the bin to stop vermin getting into it.

Q: *There are flies in the bin. What should I do?*
A: Keep a layer of cardboard on top of the bin.

Q: *Does the compost bin need to sit on soil?*
A: Yes. Worms live in the soil and get access to the bin that way.

Q: *What is the difference between wormeries and compost bins?*
A: A wormery can be kept indoors and worms are added. The liquid and the castings make excellent fertiliser.

Q: *Where should we place the bin?*
A: It should be sited in a corner of the playground where it will not cause an obstruction and on top of soil so that the worms can get in. As the materials begin to break down different mini-beasts will appear in the bin, providing a fabulous educational experience for pupils.

Q: *What do I do with the compost once we have made it?*
A: Spread it on your playing fields or use it on flowerbeds and vegetable patches. Legislation means you cannot take this off the school premises.

Take action

- Composting
- Compost in a bottle supporting classroom lesson
- Reducing lunch waste campaign.

Keep measurements logged in the eco-folder to show that the school is evaluating its performance and displaying good environmental practice.

Project 1: composting

This project involves starting up a compost bin and a system that maintains the effectiveness of the bin and the quality of the compost produced.

- **Action 1. Eco-Teacher:** order a compost bin.

  Contact the council, local environmental organisation or Waste Resources Action Programme at http://www.recyclenow.com/schools/compost/index.html and order a compost bin. These are often sold at discounted prices. If preferred, make your own compost heap with a few pieces of wood.

- **Action 2. Eco-Teacher:** procure 'kitchen caddies' and biodegradable bin liners.

  Order a kitchen caddy – a lidded plastic bin used to place compostable material – for each classroom that is going to compost, plus one for the staffroom and one for the dining hall. The caddies can be lined with a

The Environmental Toolkit for Teachers

biodegradable bag, which will break down inside the compost bin, so order a decent supply of these at the same time.

- **Action 3. Eco-Teacher:** read about composting.

    Familiarise yourself with how to make compost by looking at http://www. recyclenow.com/schools/compost/index.html and for a great animation on what happens inside the bin. There are techniques to making good compost such as getting the right balance of materials and getting air into the bin and, without some composting knowledge, you may end up putting in the wrong types of waste and end up with a pile of sludge which will be useless. Worse still, a mismanaged bin could permanently put people off composting.

- **Action 4. Eco-Teacher:** discuss a collection system.

    Discuss the introduction of the composting scheme with the Eco-Pupils. Agree which class should be used to trial the scheme and have the Eco-Pupils decide the following:

    - Who in the Eco-Team should collect the classroom caddy.
    - When the caddy will be collected.
    - How the collected material should be weighed.
    - How results will be recorded and fed back to the whole school.

    Inform the teacher of the class that has been selected to trial the system. Make sure that they are happy with the idea of having this caddy in the classroom.

- **Action 5. Eco-Pupils:** draw up a rota.

    Have the pupils draw up a schedule for collecting the caddies.

- **Action 6. Eco-Pupils:** talk to the trial class.

    The Eco-Pupils deliver the caddy to the trial class and give a short talk explaining what things the class should put in the caddy. They should mention the compost bin and why composting is good for the environment.

- **Action 7. Eco-Pupils:** begin the composting trial.

    The caddies should be collected according to the agreed rota and the waste weighed and data recorded. The caddy contents can then be placed in the compost bin making sure that the right balance of 'dry' and 'wet' waste is put in.

- **Action 8. Eco-Team:** review the trial.

  Review the system and prepare to extend it to other areas of the school.

- **Action 9. Eco-Team:** inform the whole school.

  The whole school should be informed that the school is recycling at least some of its organic waste. The Eco-Pupils can give a short talk to the whole school on the benefits of composting and how it works.

- **Action 10. Eco-Pupils:** begin the composting collection system across the school.

  With the selected classes furnished with a caddy and biodegradable bin liner bags, the Eco-Pupils should begin the collection system.

- **Action 11. Eco-Pupils:** weigh and record amount being collected.

  When the Eco-Pupils collect the caddies they should weigh the biodegradable bin liner bag and record the weight. The bags can then be deposited in the compost bin.

- **Action 12. Eco-Teacher:** enable teachers to teach the *compost in a bottle* lesson.

  Provide colleagues with a copy of the *compost in a bottle* lesson plan.

Supporting classroom lesson: compost in a bottle

This lesson plan can be found in *Appendix 10*. It teaches pupils what should go in a compost bin and allows them to observe the types of changes that occur inside.

Reducing food waste

Reducing food waste can be challenging, with plate leftovers, fruit, sandwich crusts, crisps, biscuits, juice, water and milk going into the bin on a daily basis. Food waste management strategies, whole-school projects, parental support and classroom lessons can, however, result in diverting a great deal of food waste from landfill.

Creating a culture where food waste is minimal requires perseverance. Project 2 overleaf can be repeated on regular occasions, even weekly, in order to keep the momentum going. Alternatively, a lunch monitor can help to promote the finishing of food. Some schools use a teacher to check that children finish all their food before leaving the lunch hall. Make sure, though, to promote encouragement rather than force, otherwise children may become apprehensive at the thought of having to eat food they really don't like.

Remember

Food can be a sensitive issue. The main concerns are health and safety, obesity and parental attitudes.

Health – One way to reduce food waste is to encourage children to eat all of their lunch. If, however, the food they have brought from home is a packet of crisps, sweets and a fizzy drink, it may be unwise to promote eating it when there are obvious health issues. The school needs a healthy eating policy and to promote consumption of healthy rather than unhealthy food.

Share trays – A share tray can be used for unwanted food. A child can place a piece of unwanted food on it for others to take if they wish to. There are issues surrounding this approach, however, with some people concerned there are health risks in eating food another person has touched.

Catering companies – Catering firms are often contracted to prepare and serve school lunches. The menu they set is usually for a month and the amount of food prepared is based on the number of children that have ordered a school lunch. Generally speaking, the companies produce good, nutritious food, but inevitably there will be days when the menu contains a dish that some of the pupils don't like and extra waste will occur. Solutions should be sought to minimise this waste.

Liquids – People often forget that liquid left in cartons goes to landfill too, so remind pupils to drink up.

Parents – Parents like to know if their child has eaten all their lunch. Any unfinished food from a home packed lunch should go back to the parents so that they are aware of their child's food habits. Parents can be reminded that food waste is a problem and that they should try to make a lunch which is both nutritious and that their child is likely to eat.

Staff – The staff can exemplify good food habits and a share tray may work in the staffroom.

Project 2: reducing lunch waste campaign

This campaign tackles school lunch waste by following a clear engagement process. Lunchtime food waste is weighed before the whole school is engaged to tackle the problem.

Remember

If some pupils can't or won't eat all their food, then they should be encouraged just to eat as much as they can.

The school catering company also has a part to play as they may have ideas on how to keep leftover food waste to a minimum, so get them involved in the campaign too.

- **Action 1. Eco-Team:** audit school lunch waste.

  Conduct an audit by weighing the food waste bins after one lunch. Include classroom bins if packed lunches are eaten there. Record the total weight and use as evidence to start the campaign.

- **Action 2. Eco-Teacher:** seek permission from senior staff.

  Seek permission to tackle the school food waste issue. The head teacher should be made aware that consent will be sought from parents asking them to support a campaign to have the pupils 'clear their plate' at lunchtime.

- **Action 3. Eco-Teacher:** meet the caterer.

  Meet the caterer and ask if they have any ideas on how they could help reduce food waste. Some suggestions might be reviewing portion sizes and improving the way the food is advertised (for example, making dish names more fun).

- **Action 4. Eco-Team:** prepare a whole-school gathering talk.

  Using evidence from the food waste audit, the Eco-Team should prepare a whole-school gathering talk about food waste in the school.

The talk should contain:

- the results from the audit
- evidence of untouched food
- a picture of a landfill site.

- **Action 5. Eco-Teacher:** set a date for encouraging children to reduce food waste.

  Identify a date when the whole school will be involved in trying to reduce its lunch waste.

- **Action 6. Eco-Pupils:** give a whole-school presentation.

  After the Eco-Pupils have practised their presentation, they should give the talk to the whole school.

- **Action 7. Eco-Teacher:** prepare rewards.

  Prepare for the big day by sourcing stickers or other items that will reward the pupils that try their best to clear their plates.

- **Action 8. Eco-Team:** hold reduce lunch waste day.

  On an identified day, remind the diners that they must try to finish all the food on their plates. Walk among the diners encouraging them and issue the rewards to those children that try to eat all their food. If packed lunches are eaten in classrooms, classroom assistants, the Eco-Pupils or teachers can do the encouraging.

- **Action 9. Eco-Pupils:** measuring and recording the waste.

  At the end of lunch, the team, as in the initial audit, should weigh each bag of food waste and record the findings. The result should be that the weight is less than the initial audit.

- **Action 10. Eco-Team:** celebrate.

  Share the findings at a whole-school gathering and post the recording sheets on the eco-noticeboard for parents and visitors to see.

Packaging

Packaging waste includes cardboard, plastics, tetrapacks, foil, glass and metal. Implementing packaging recycling systems and finding opportunities to reuse and reduce packaging waste are explored through familiar waste management strategies and projects such as the waste-free packed lunch. Supporting classroom lessons include the fun *egg packaging* activity.

Recycling packaging

Some local councils provide a packaging recycling collection for their schools, but for those schools that don't, one must be arranged with a recycling collection company. Most recycling companies will collect cardboard, plastics, glass and tetrapacks, but as glass and metal do not account for much school waste, there may be little need for arranging a collection of these materials. A staff member may bring in an occasional can or tin at lunchtime but these can be taken home and recycled domestically.

Remember

Milk cartons should be washed out before they are collected and the implication for the school is that it has to wash out potentially hundreds of smelly milk cartons!

Cardboard is recycled back into cardboard, glass into glass and metal back to metal. Plastics can be made into other plastic goods or into the fleece material used in clothing or loft insulation. Tetrapacks can also be turned into a variety of products, such as clipboards.

Frequently asked questions

Q: *How do I know if something is paper or card?*
A: If it rips, it is paper. If it tears, leaving thicker fibres at the edge, then it is card.

Q: *What gets made from recycled plastic?*
A: More plastic goods, pencils, pens, fleeces and insulation material.

Q: *How do I know if the plastic is recyclable?*
A: Ask your recycling collection company or check the packaging.

Take action

- Packaging recycling system
- Egg packaging supporting classroom lesson.

Project 1: packaging recycling system

This project organises to have plastics, cardboard and other packaging material collected from the school and sets up a system where pupils can collect materials ready to be uplifted.

- **Action 1. Eco-Teacher:** arrange a packaging recycling collection.

  Contact the waste department at your local council to enquire about arranging packaging recycling collections for the school, asking:

  - What materials can be collected?
  - What are the arrangements for a collection?
  - How much does a packaging collection cost?
  - Can tetrapacks can be collected and, if so, do they need to be washed out?

  Shop around for prices from other local recycling collection companies.

- **Action 2. Eco-Teacher:** approach the business manager.

  With the information you have gathered, approach the school business manager and ask if the school will pay for such a collection.

- **Action 3. Eco-Team:** plan a packaging recycling collection system.

  Plan how to collect the packaging in school. A bin may be required at 'hot spots' such as the lunch hall for bottles, cartons and yoghurt pots, and the office for cardboard boxes.

- **Action 4. Eco-Team:** milk carton recycling collection plan.

  Milk cartons are recyclable, but the recycling company may require these to be clean before they collect them. The Eco-Team should meet to plan a system for how the cleaning will be undertaken. Potential solutions are:

  - Asking each individual or each class to wash out their own cartons.
  - Having the Eco-Pupils wash out cartons one day a week.

- Only collecting a practical number of cartons. Recycling some is better than none.

Remember to encourage pupils to drink all their milk; the more they do the less ends up in landfill.

- **Action 5. Eco-Teacher:** plan to compost cardboard.

   Explain to the Eco-Pupils that cardboard is to be collected for adding to the compost bin. Ask the pupils where in the school they might find quantities of card. Elicit that some comes in the form of cardboard boxes that are delivered to the school. The most likely people to take delivery of this type of material are the school caretaker and office staff. The pupils should plan how to collect this material.

- **Action 6. Eco-Pupils:** collect cardboard for composting.

   The Eco-Pupils should collect cardboard from around the school on a regular basis. Once collected, it should be cut up and added to the compost bin.

- **Action 7. Eco-Teacher:** metal and glass recycling.

   Make staff aware that, if they bring cans, tins or glass containers to work, they should take them home and recycle them domestically. This will avoid the need to arrange a collection for these materials.

Supporting classroom lesson: egg packaging

To support the understanding of packaging waste, a practical activity is the *egg packaging* lesson. This allows pupils to explore the nature of packaging and teaches them how it can be reduced, reused and recycled. The lesson plan is set out in *Appendix 11*.

Reusing packaging

Many types of packaging material can be easily reused. Card, plastics, metal and glass can usually be reused as practical items or as material for art and craft lessons. Reuse opportunities should be identified, robust collection systems put in place and the collected material weighed regularly as a measure of how much packaging waste the school is diverting from landfill.

Reusing packaging materials not only improves environmental performance but can save the school money by reducing the need to buy new items.

Remember

There may be a limit to the number of plastic bottles, glass jars or cardboard boxes that can be reused in the school, so non-reusable material should be recycled.

Note also that materials may not be recyclable after they have been painted or glued. A few ideas for promoting reuse of packaging materials are as follows:

- cardboard box = storage box for books or folders
- plastic ice cream container = stationery holder
- plastic takeaway food box = sandwich box
- plastic bottle = water bottle
- cereal packet = tray
- plastic bag = bag for storing fabric

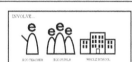

Take action

- Packaging reuse
- Making a pen holder from a milk carton supporting classroom lesson
- The plastic bottle greenhouse.

Cardboard boxes, bottles and plastic trays can be given a practical second life by imaginative pupils.

Project 1: packaging reuse

In this project, surplus packaging is reused for practical purposes.

- **Action 1. Eco-Team:** assess reuse options.

  Meet to assess what packaging materials could be collected for reuse and how much needs to be collected, as there may be a limit to the amount of cardboard or plastic that can be reused.

- **Action 2. Eco-Team:** consider the collection frequency.

  After the reuse assessment has taken place, consider how often the selected materials should be collected – you might end up with more than you know what to do with; for example, there may be hundreds of yoghurt pots in the school every day but only a few needed for a seed-growing lesson.

- **Action 3. Eco-Pupils:** implement the collection system.

  Implement the system by collecting the required amounts of material at the agreed frequency rate. Once the material has been collected the Eco-Pupils can place it in storage for later reuse.

- **Action 4. Eco-Pupils:** weigh and record collected amounts.

  After each round of collections, weigh the material and record the amount. Log the data in the eco-folder.

Supporting classroom lesson: making a pencil holder from a milk carton

Provide classroom teachers with the lesson plan notes on *Making a pencil holder from a milk carton* found in *Appendix 12*.

Project 2: the plastic bottle greenhouse

This is a project that puts plastic bottles to great use by fitting them to a wooden frame to make a greenhouse. See http://www.reapscotland.org.uk on how to undertake this project.

Reducing packaging

Packaging waste reduction requires an understanding of who brings packaging into the school and engaging with that person or organisation. The main sources of packaging waste are likely to be caterers, school equipment suppliers, pupils, parents and staff. It is important to understand how and where this waste is produced and by whom tobe able to tackle the waste at source.

Remember

The project assumes there are at least some pupils bringing packed lunches to school and that the parents will be supportive of the project.

Take action

- The waste-free packed lunch
- Caterers
- Suppliers
- School Staff
- The pledge hedge project.

Project 1: the waste-free packed lunch

Much of the packaging waste in school is brought in via pupils' packed lunches made at home. This project aims to reduce waste by encouraging parents to prepare packed lunches that contain as little packaging as possible. The actions include planning the project, measuring the extent of packed lunch waste and engaging parents to help reduce that waste.

- **Action 1. Eco-Team:** plan the project.

  Plan how to measure the weight of packaging waste from packed lunches. Consider where packed lunches are normally eaten (for example, classrooms or dining hall).

- **Action 2. Eco-Pupils:** make signs for rubbish bags.

  Make a sign for each type of waste that is going to be collected at lunchtime: food, liquids, plastic bottles, cartons, wrappers, yoghurt pots and cardboard. (The signs will be placed beside the different rubbish bags.)

- **Action 3. Eco-Teacher:** meet catering staff.

  Inform the catering staff that the Eco-Team are going to collect packed lunch packaging waste in separate bags for one day to find out if the school can reduce its waste. Assure the staff that this won't require any extra work on their part.

- **Action 4. Eco-Teacher:** inform colleagues and diners.

  Inform staff that there will be a slight disruption at lunchtime as the Eco-Team are going to collect the waste in different bags.

- **Action 5. Eco-Team:** collect classroom packed lunch waste.

  If packed lunches are eaten in classrooms, give each class the task of placing their packaging waste in a separate bin bag for that day.

- **Action 6. Eco-Team:** collect packed lunch packaging waste.

  Before lunch the Eco-Team should assemble in the dining hall and be ready to guide the diners on where to place packed lunch rubbish. The Eco-Team should source a plastic bin liner for each type of waste to be collected and stick the signs they made on the bags. A basin should be sourced for collecting any liquids. When packed lunch diners finish their lunch they should place any rubbish in the correct bag/basin.

- **Action 7. Eco-Pupils:** measure the collected waste and record findings.

  After the waste has been collected, the pupils should measure the weight of each bag using a spring balance or set of scales. Record the results.

- **Action 8. Eco-Pupils:** share results.

  Share the results with the rest of the school via the eco-noticeboard

- **Action 9. Eco-Team:** engage parents.

  Inform the parents of the results of the audit and ask them to help reduce packaging waste at the school by minimising the amount of plastic and other materials in the packed lunches they prepare.

Project 2: caterers

School caterers are often contracted to supply school lunches. These lunches are often prepared at a central location and arrive in school in packaging materials, such as plastic from sandwich boxes, plastic wrappers and cartons. In order to reduce this type of waste a discussion between the school and the catering firm needs to take place.

- **Action 1. Eco-Teacher:** meet the caterer.

  Explain to the caterer that the school is trying to reduce packaging waste. Discuss ideas on how this could be achieved. Potential solutions are for them to supply juice in large cartons and yoghurt in large pots rather than in individual size versions. The contents can be decanted into glasses, which are washed and used again.

The caterer may explain the reasons for the styles of packaging used, but discuss whether larger cartons may be more cost-effective for them as well as helping to prevent waste in school.

Project 3: suppliers

When suppliers deliver goods to the school, packaging materials such as cardboard, plastic and polystyrene may enter into the waste stream. Suppliers may have a policy of recovering packaging from their customers and so you may be able to return the packaging material to the company or council that delivered it.

- **Action 1. Eco-Teacher:** seek advice on returning packaging.

  Seek advice from the education department or waste services department on returning packaging to suppliers.

- **Action 2. Eco-Teacher:** contact school equipment suppliers.

  Contact school equipment suppliers to discuss if they would be willing to take back the packaging materials and get them recycled.

Project 4: school staff

Staff should aim to exemplify the school environmental ethos and reduce their own personal packaging waste and there are several ways to do this:

- Buy shared items, such as tea, coffee, milk and juice, in bulk. This could be more cost-effective as well as less wasteful.
- Keep any plastic bags for others to reuse.
- Take packaging home to recycle domestically.
- Use plastic containers rather than foil or polythene wrapping.
- Bring in home-made cakes rather than bought cakes.

- **Action 1. Eco-Teacher:** meet staff.

  Hold a short meeting to discuss how the staff could prevent packaging waste. Suggest the options above and agree on their implementation.

Project 5: the pledge hedge

This project can be used to engage the community in reducing packaging waste by asking people to avoid buying goods that are over-packaged. If people adopt these actions then they will generate less rubbish, which will have a positive impact on the surrounding environment. School pupils will ask their parents to commit to these pro-environmental behaviours and sign a *pledge leaf* which the school can then display, creating a large 'hedge' of pledges.

Remember

The project relies on the support and will of the community to engage in these issues.

- **Action 1. Eco-Team:** plan the project.

  Outline the project to the Eco-Pupils. Explain that they are going to visit each class in school and issue all the pupils with a *pledge hedge leaf*. The leaf forms part of the campaign to reduce waste in the community. The pupils in each class take a leaf home to be read by parents and signed if they agree to reduce packaging waste. The leaves will then be returned to the school and put on display. The Eco-Pupils should plan how best to distribute, collect and display the leaves.

- **Action 2. Eco-Teacher:** make pledge leaves.

  Print enough copies of the pledge leaf for each household to be engaged. See *Appendix 13*.

- **Action 3. Eco-Team:** explain *the pledge hedge project* to pupils.

  The Eco-Team visit each class in the school and explain *the pledge hedge project*. They issue each child with a leaf and ask for it to be signed and returned within one week.

- **Action 4. Eco-Team:** collect the leaves.

  A box for returned pledge leaves can be left at the school entrance or, alternatively, the Eco-Team could collect them from each class. Once they are collected and counted, the number should be recorded in the eco-folder as evidence of engagement with the local community.

- **Action 5. Eco-Team:** display the leaves.

  Display some or all of the leaves on the school eco-noticeboard in the shape of a hedge.

Resource efficiency and recycled procurement

Resource efficiency in school is about using equipment, such as stationery and books, to their fullest potential use. To avoid needless waste, these resources need to be looked after carefully and so the school must create an ethos of care and responsibility towards resource use. Adopting a whole-school policy that commits everyone to care for school resources will help in creating a culture of responsibility. There are practical activities that the Eco-Team can also carry out.

Take action

- Respect our resources campaign
- Found tray
- Repair workshop.

These projects work best if you begin with the campaign, as this highlights the issue, and then move on to the next two projects. With school resources being looked after to this extent, the school will create an ethos of care and responsibility towards resource use and the Eco-Pupils will have learned valuable campaigning and repair skills.

Project 1: respect our resources campaign

The campaign aims to address resource neglect by following the 4 E principles (see Encouraging sustainable behaviour change in Chapter 1 for details) to change people's behaviours using engagement techniques.

- **Action 1. Eco-Team:** plan the campaign.

  Discuss 'resource neglect' and then ask the pupils to identify examples of efficient practice. Tell them they are going to promote good resource efficiency by engaging their peers through a campaign. Ask them how they would go about getting other pupils to look after their things. Elicit ideas

Taking action on waste

such as a school talk, posters or a song. Make a plan using the ideas put forward.

- **Action 2. Eco-Teacher:** engage staff.

  Engage the staff by explaining the need for resource efficiency. Ask them to help implement a whole-school policy to make sure pupils look after equipment. Mention that the Eco-Team will be launching the *respect our resources* campaign. Allow time for any questions.

- **Action 3. Eco-Teacher:** set policy with management.

  Meet with management to set a policy that states that everyone in the school must respect school equipment and resources and use them as effectively and efficiently as possible.

- **Action 4. Eco-Pupils:** make campaign posters.

  Campaign posters promoting positive resource behaviours should be made to help engage the school pupils.

- **Action 5. Eco-Pupils:** engage the whole school.

  The Eco-Pupils should talk to the whole school during a whole-school gathering, introducing the *respect our resources* campaign. The talk should include how inefficient use of resources is wasteful. The resources that are to be looked after include anything the pupils use in school, such as books, pencils, paint, etc. Examples of efficient behaviour should be highlighted.

- **Action 6. Eco-Team:** encourage the whole school.

  Encourage everyone by offering a prize or reward to individuals that use equipment efficiently. Maintain momentum by offering the incentive at regular intervals throughout the school term.

Project 2: found tray

A *found tray* is for equipment that has been found in school and can include pencils, pen lids, glue sticks or anything that still has a use. The Eco-Pupils could run this as part of an 'Eco-Shop' and give out the equipment to anyone that has a use for it.

- **Action 1. Eco-Teacher:** explain the project.

  Meet with the Eco-Team and explain the *found tray* project. Ask them to source a suitable tray and to decorate it suitably.

- **Action 2. Eco-Team:** discuss and organize the project.

  Discuss how the *found tray* should be organized and run. Areas to consider:

  - Where the found tray should be located
  - When the found tray should be available (all the time, or just some of it)
  - Whether there will be Eco-Pupils present (if the *found tray* is only available some of the time), or if the tray will be left unattended.

- **Action 3. Eco-Team:** engage with school.

  The Eco-Team should go each class and explain the concept.

- **Action 4. Eco-Team:** run the project.

  Run the *found tray* project as agreed, reviewing how it is working at pre-arranged intervals.

- **Action 5. Eco-Teacher:** contact cleaners.

  Cleaners should be made aware of the *found tray* as they often find equipment while cleaning.

Project 3: repair workshop

Damaged equipment can be repaired at a 'repair workshop' run by the Eco-Pupils. The equipment needing attention may include broken pencils, pens without lids, erasers that need cleaning or books that need stapling back together.

- **Action 1. Eco-Team:** advertise the 'repair workshop'.

  Advertise the existence of the 'repair workshop' using posters in classrooms or a talk at a whole-school gathering. The advertising material should state what type of broken equipment the Eco-Team are able to repair. Mention that pupils can hand in equipment to the Eco-Team.

- **Action 2. Eco-Team:** repair equipment.

  Run the 'repair workshop' as often as is needed, repairing and redistributing equipment as appropriate.

Recycled procurement

An important aspect of the waste hierarchy is procuring recycled goods because buying recycled products creates a demand for them, so try to buy what recycled goods you can. Paper, pencils, pens, rulers, clipboards, hand towels and toilet paper are just some of the recycled goods that can be purchased.

Remember

Some people have concerns that recycled goods are not as good as those made from virgin materials; for example, that photocopiers do not take recycled paper or recycled pencils break more easily. There is no evidence I am aware of that supports these theories but be sympathetic to people's fears and simply test materials if they are questioned and draw your own conclusions.

Take action

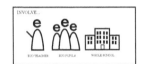

- Buy recycled
- Equipment amnesty

Buying recycled goods is an element of the Eco-Schools programme, so the school's efforts to establish a sustainable procurement policy will help gain Green Flag status. An amnesty reduces the need to buy equipment that the school already has and is an example of good housekeeping.

Project 1: buy recycled

The aim is to create a school policy on buying recycled products.

- **Action 1. Eco-Teacher:** research recycled alternatives.

  Research the web to find suppliers of recycled products. Some websites worth looking at are:

  - Stationery – http://www.remarkable.co.uk

- Office supplies – http://www.thegreenoffice.co.uk.

Contact companies for prices.

- **Action 2. Eco-Teacher:** research recycling procurement possibilities.

  Meet the business manager to discuss the school's purchasing policy. Suggest that the school fulfil its own environmental policy and commit itself to buying recycled goods wherever possible. Supply the manager with the prices of recycled paper, pencils and other stationery researched earlier.

- **Action 3. Eco-Teacher:** meet the school management.

  Meet the school management to discuss the budget implications for purchasing recycled products. Get agreement that the school can begin to procure the identified goods.

Project 2: equipment amnesty

An *equipment amnesty* is an aspect of efficient resource practice. The amnesty works by asking pupils and staff to hand in any extra equipment they have but perhaps don't use. A teacher, for example, may find that he/she has two staplers when only one is needed, so the extra item is handed in. Once the extra equipment has been collected, it can be redistributed to others according to need.

- **Action 1. Eco-Team:** plan action.

  Plan an *equipment amnesty* to make best use of the resources within the school.

- **Action 2. Eco-Pupils:** engage teachers and pupils.

  Communicate with each class and ask them to look through cupboards and drawers to find any unused stationery equipment.

- **Action 3. Eco-Pupils:** collect equipment.

  Once each class has collected any extra equipment, the Eco-Pupils can gather it together, sort it into categories (for example, staplers, sticky tape, pens etc.) and return it to the stationery cupboard.

There are many ways to minimise waste in school. Implementing the projects listed in this chapter will result in a waste-free school, something for the school to be extremely proud of. Schools don't become waste-free overnight because these waste actions take time to put into operation. But if the tasks are allocated and shared among the Eco-Team, pupils and staff then progress will be made more quickly.

Auditing, monitoring and evaluating are key aspects of environmental management, so the projects that are undertaken should be reviewed regularly to ensure that the systems in place follow good practice and are working effectively. Enabling, engaging, exemplifying and encouraging are the cornerstones of real, sustainable behaviour change, and these concepts should be applied to any waste project whether the context is packaging, paper or food.

Good school housekeeping includes good waste management practice and the school should adopt policies for ethical procurement and resource efficiency. An *equipment amnesty* can be a good way to kick-start a campaign to make the school more resource efficient.

End of chapter references

1 Department for Food and Rural Affairs (2012), 'UK Waste Data', Department for Food and Rural Affairs. Available from: http://www.defra.gov.uk/statistics/environment/waste/wrfg01-annsector/ (Accessed 08/03/13).

2 Waste Watch (2005), 'Resource management in the education sector'. London, p.10.

3 WRAP (2008), 'The Nature and Scale of Waste produced by Schools in England'. Banbury, p. 2.

4 Waste Watch (2011), 'Wacky Waste Facts' Waste Watch. Available from: http://www.wastewatch.org.uk (Accessed 08/03/13).

5 Waste Watch (2011), 'Statistics' DEFRA. Available from: http://www.wasteonline.org.uk/searchresults?Classification=Statistics&Keywords=paper%26cardboard (Accessed 08/03/2013).

6 WRAP (2008), 'Report into the Nature and Scale of Waste produced by Schools in England'. Banbury, p.7.

7 WRAP (2011), 'Food Waste in Schools'. Banbury, p.5.

4 Taking action on energy

Introduction to energy management

Energy is mostly generated by the carbon-based fuels oil, coal and natural gas and every time an electrical or gas appliance is used, carbon dioxide is released into the atmosphere contributing to global warming. The largest element of a school's environmental footprint is the energy used to power its heating, lighting and small power machines and, therefore, energy can be deemed as one of the most important areas of environmental management that a school should address.

Energy management is the process of monitoring, controlling and conserving energy use and is a discipline that can significantly reduce carbon emissions. To help promote energy conservation in schools, a European Directive stipulates that schools over $1000m^2$ must obtain a certificate rating their energy usage. To achieve a good rating practical measures are required, including measuring consumption, regularly maintaining equipment, implementing conserving measures and promoting positive behaviours. These principles apply to the use of heating systems, lighting, computers and monitors and anything else that consumes energy in the school.

Eco-Schools and energy

The energy topic is compulsory for Eco-Schools in England and actions should be built around the framework of the seven elements of an Eco-Schools programme including a review or in this case an energy audit, which must be carried out, and an action plan created based on the findings. See How to implement environmental management in Chapter 1. With these elements in place, an energy programme can be implemented across the whole school.

There are many actions within a school energy management programme and each project or campaign should involve the whole school so that all the pupils and staff are aware of the reasons for reducing energy use and their role in making it happen.

Table 6 Typical actions of a good energy management system

Action	Description
Record figures	Take a meter reading for gas and electricity at the beginning and end of one school day to establish a benchmark
Photographs and evidence	Show your work in a file
Monitor and evaluate	Once you have a benchmark energy consumption figure, begin to take regular meter readings
	Analyse findings to see if projects and interventions have had an impact
	Record the number of people engaged in your campaigns
Involve the community where possible	Encourage parents to get involved at home

The steps involved in implementing these actions are set out in the next section, but a good starting point for any energy project is to conduct a whole-school energy audit.

Know your energy

Knowing what you can and what you cannot influence is important at the outset of energy projects. There are several issues that affect how much a school Eco-Team can influence energy consumption in their own building.

Control

The first issue that school Eco-Teams may face is the amount of control over heating and lighting. These systems may be centrally controlled by a building energy management system (BEMS) that regulate the building's heating and lighting for a more effective level of consumption.

Another factor is that the most significant reductions in energy consumption are achieved by investment in large-scale, structural changes such as glazing, movement detectors and insulation measures and these changes require the financial support of the local authority. Many school buildings are old and the high cost of introducing improvements means that the school may be unable to make the required changes that have the most significant impacts.

Lack of control also extends to the gas and electricity being used by caterers, caretakers, cleaners and community groups that use the building out of school hours. These people must also be engaged in campaigns in order to maximise the number of people involved and to reduce usage further. A common issue is that cleaners leave lights switched on but, because they have not been engaged, they are unaware of the school campaign to save energy.

Money

Saving money can be as much of a motivation as reducing emissions. It is estimated that good energy housekeeping can reduce a school's fuel bills by 20%[1] and that can mean several hundred pounds to a small primary school. This acts as an added incentive for school business managers. However, there is sometimes the problem that financial savings are not always passed on to the school.

Technology versus environment

The use of small power machines such as smart boards, computers, monitors, printers and other electrical appliances is increasing. Though there are great educational benefits for using such technology, the electricity they consume poses a problem for reducing overall energy consumption. Some schools agree rules and systems on how and when such appliances should be switched off or put on stand-by in order to save energy.

Efficiency before renewables

Energy efficiency should be tackled ahead of renewable energy projects, such as wind turbines or solar panels. Installing a wind turbine may be a more exciting project than draught-proofing windows, but the latter is often more effective.

- Space heating accounts for 60% of school energy use.[2]
- Lighting accounts for 20% of energy expenditure.[3]
- Electrical equipment accounts 3% of use and 5% of expenditure.[4]
- Teaching areas should be 18° C and 15°C in corridors.[5]
- Hot water temperature should be set at 60°C as this is the temperature that kills germs.
- The level of UK primary energy consumption in 2011 was 5% lower than 1990.[6]
- Monitors use more energy than the computer itself.
- Energy can be created from waste by using methane as a fuel.
- Ground source heat pumps provide natural heat by taking pipes under the ground.
- A 3mm gap around a door is equivalent to a hole the size of a brick.[7]

Resources for energy management

There are an overwhelming number of energy management documents and resources to help schools reduce energy. The key resources are listed below under the headings, *Energy management*, *Teaching tools* and *Energy devices*.

Energy management

- The Carbon Trust is a key organisation that has produced a series of energy management leaflets for schools as well as free posters and stickers. They also conduct energy and footprinting audits. http://www.carbontrust.com/resources/guides/sector-based-advice/schools.

- The Energy Saving Trust gives tips for householders, communities and schools. The EST provides excellent energy management advice and information on accessing funding. http://www.energysavingtrust.org.uk/funding.

- Carbon Detectives allow you to register and join their certification programme. You can use the carbon and energy footprint calculator as the starting point of your campaign. http://www.carbondetectiveseurope.org.

- Energy Benchmarking lets you benchmark your school energy and compare it to other schools through this online tool. http://www. energybenchmarking.co.uk/schools/default.asp.

Teaching tools

- Join the Pod provides lesson plans and a campaign backed by Eco-Schools. http://www.jointhepod.org
- British Gas gives useful whole-school gathering and teacher notes, including material on insulation. http://www.generationgreen.co.uk.
- CREATE has various links to lesson plans and energy management tools. http://www.create.org.uk/schools/teachers_resources.asp.

Energy devices

- Your local authority energy management team may have a guide to managing energy in schools and they may be able to supply supporting campaign tools such as posters or even plugs, light bulbs or energy monitoring meters.
- Eco Style has a range of eco friendly gadgets. http://www.ecostyle.co.uk/ products.html.
- The Green Button provides schools with a Green IT power-saving schedule and automatically powers down the school's computers at times that they are not being used. http://thegreenbuttoncampaign.com/.

Understanding school energy management

The key elements that make up a successful school energy management programme include the following:

- An energy policy
- An Eco-Team
- Regular energy auditing
- Getting buy-in from head teachers, caretakers and catering staff
- Writing an action plan
- Monitoring and evaluating consumption
- Involving the whole school and wider community.

First, a written energy policy shows others that you are making a commitment and this helps to keep pupils inspired, especially if they have helped to write it. The Eco-Team are key to delivering the commitment and should be fully aware of the need to reduce energy consumption, understanding what are positive and negative energy behaviours. Positive energy behaviours are those that save energy, such as switching a light off whilst negative energy behaviours are those that waste energy unnecessarily, such as leaving a light on in an unoccupied room. The team can take this learning and put it to use by conducting an energy audit; identifying areas where the school could improve its performance in the areas of heating, lighting and the use of small power machines. The Eco-Team should also be responsible for taking regular meter readings to monitor how much energy the school uses. During the audit the Eco-Team can discuss the positive energy behaviours that should be promoted and create a campaign which will help remove barriers to negative energy habits among pupils and staff.

At this point, getting key people on board is important. Head teachers and business managers can sanction expenditure and caretakers have practical skills in maintenance, an important aspect of an energy-efficient school. Caterers, too, should be involved as their behaviours could reduce carbon impact. Engaging these people early in any campaign will help overcome the obstacles to positive energy behaviours.

Frequently asked questions

Q: *What appliances use most power?*
A: Heating and lighting consume most power in a typical school.

Q: *Does switching off a light and then on again use more energy than keeping it left on?*
A: No. Switching on an energy saving bulb only uses the same amount of power as leaving it on for a minute or two.

Q: *How do you calculate the energy an appliance uses?*
A: Multiply the product of wattage and hours per day by the number of days the device is used per year. (Watts x Hours per day x Days used per year). Divide the result of (Watts x Hours per day x Days used per year) by 1000. This gives you the total power consumption per year in kWh. The formula used is: (Watts x Hours per day x Days per year) ÷ 1000 = kWh.

Q: *Lights in the gym hall have to be left on because they take a long time to warm up. Is that ok?*
A: Consult your local authority energy management team for advice.

Getting started with energy management

Getting started in energy management involves putting in place systems for regularly auditing and measuring energy consumption, which are essential elements of good energy management practice. These tasks can be implemented through projects that include energy auditing, meter reading and getting others engaged.

The projects involve the Eco-Team conducting an audit of the school identifying where energy is being wasted, either through structural deficiencies or by behaviours of the pupils and staff. You can use the findings from this audit to inform the action planning stage where it is decided how consumption is to be reduced. Meter readings should be regularly recorded from this point onwards to build an understanding of how much energy is being used in the school. The Eco-Pupils can perform this task initially, but it can then be shared among other children so that more of the school is involved.

It is also good to involve the home at the beginning of an energy topic. Parents can raise their energy awareness by taking meter readings and auditing their own homes. The projects set out in this chapter explain how to get these projects underway.

Take action

- Energy audit
- Energy habits supporting classroom lesson
- Meter readers
- Home energy checks.

By auditing, recording and measuring regularly the school will be better informed about its energy consumption.

Project 1: energy audit

The Eco-Pupils act as detectives discovering where energy is being wasted across the school. They identify structural issues, such as room temperatures, drips, leaks and draughts, as well as behavioural issues such as lights and machines being left on unnecessarily. Using various tools the pupils record their findings.

- **Action 1. Eco-Teacher:** seek assistance.

Contact your local authority energy management team and explain that the school is going to measure its energy demand through meter reading. Ask if they can provide support and assistance.

- **Action 2. Eco-Teacher:** research audit tools.

  Become familiar with auditing tools such as checklists and calculators. Read the audit advice provided by the Carbon Trust and review the carbon calculator at http://www.carbondetectiveseurope.org/Country. aspx?CountryID=10. Also look at the http://www.energybenchmarking.co.uk website to see what information will help provide a benchmark. Also check http://www.jointhepod.org for resources.

- **Action 3. Eco-Teacher:** discuss with the Eco-Team.

  Meet with the Eco-Team and discuss the audit purpose and process. Explain the audit worksheets and tools you have chosen. Ask the caretaker and any other available adults to help with the audit.

- **Action 4. Eco-Team:** conduct audit.

  Use the audit guidance in *Appendix 14.*

- **Action 5. Eco-Team:** analyse findings.

  When the group returns, discuss the findings. They will have identified areas of energy wastage.

- **Action 6. Eco-Team:** enter results.

  With results from the audit, feed these into benchmark and carbon calculator website tools.

- **Action 7. Eco-Team:** conclusion.

  From the analysis, begin to form the basis for a plan of action. Decide whether to tackle structural issues or behavioural issues. Consider heating and lighting as a priority and read the relevant chapters from this book.

Supporting classroom lesson: energy habits

After hearing about the energy audit, pupils in their classrooms can investigate positive energy habits.

Project 2: meter readers

In this project pupils record the figures shown on the school's gas and electricity meters so that they can see how much is being used per day. This helps the school benchmark its performance. This should be done every day and analysed regularly to be able to show the pattern of energy demand. The local authority energy management team may be able to provide support for the project.

- **Action 1. Eco-Team:** meet caretaker.

  Ask for assistance from the caretaker, as he or she will know where the meters are and how to read them.

- **Action 2. Eco-Pupils:** record figures.

  Record the meter readings, noting the time they are read. Try to read these at the same time each day in order to get an accurate picture of daily energy consumption.

- **Action 3. Eco-Pupils:** repeat.

  Recording consumption every hour helps to build a picture of consumption. Read at the beginning and end of the day. Continue this for a week.

- **Action 4. Eco-Team:** analyse and graph.

  Graph the meter readings to provide a visual of energy consumption. Look for times through the day where demand has peaked. Look out for consumption patterns before and after school hours too. These are times when cleaners and others consume energy.

- **Action 5. Eco-Pupils:** draw up rota.

  Get others in the school involved in the project. Draw up a rota for other classes to help with the readings.

Project 3: home energy checks

This community project engages parents through recording their domestic energy meter readings and completing an online Home Energy Check. Pupils write a letter explaining how and why energy awareness is important and the whole school gets involved in taking the letters home. The number of households that take part is recorded and used as evidence of engaging with the community.

- **Action 1. Eco-Pupils:** draft letter to parents.

  Have pupils write a letter explaining the school's energy saving campaign and asking parents to join the school's energy campaign by calculating their carbon footprint using http://carboncalculator.direct.gov.uk/index.html.

- **Action 2. Eco-Pupils:** present to whole school.

  Hand out the letters to pupils at a whole-school gathering. Ask that parents return a tear-off slip showing that they are taking part.

- **Action 3. Eco-Pupils**: collect the replies.

  The replies should be collected a week later and the number of positive replies recorded.

- **Action 4. Eco-Pupils:** report, thank and celebrate.

  After all the replies have been received, a notice should be placed on the eco-noticeboard thanking all those that took part and showing the number of people that replied.

Heating

This section looks at two of the most significant impacts on school ecological impact: space heating and water heating, and sets out the actions that the Eco-Team and the whole school can take to implement good heating management practice. Bear in mind that the space heating project is best done in the colder months of the year when the heating system is used.

Space heating

Space heating has by far the largest impact on schools' ecological footprints, because of the amount of fuel required to power the heating system and inadequate insulation resulting in much of the generated heat escaping through walls, windows and doors. Antiquated heating systems, large spaces to heat and badly positioned radiators are other structural factors that can affect heating efficiency in a school building. These are big issues to tackle, but there is still much that can be done to reduce heat wastage.

Understanding your school heating system and adopting procedures that make most effective use of it can make a difference to consumption levels.

Your heating system may be controlled either centrally by the local authority or it may be managed on site by the caretaker who manages the boiler, checks that pipes are maintained and that the system is working efficiently. Whatever the system in place, the Eco-Team should carry out routine management tasks such as:

- Carrying out a heat audit of the school building.
- Reading meters.
- Measuring and reporting room temperatures (DfES Guidance 0029/2000 Standards for School premises state that rooms should be18 °C and corridors 15 °C).
- Reporting hot and cold spots.
- Helping to identify and fix draughts.

Engaging people in behaviours such as keeping windows closed in winter, avoiding use of electrical heaters and wearing appropriate clothing is a necessary part of space heating management, and the following projects can fully involve the Eco-Team and the get whole school on board with space heating management.

Remember

Children experience temperature differently from adults so take their needs into account. Rooms that are too hot affect concentration and performance. Be aware of heat that comes from computers, other small power machines and lighting. These all contribute to the overall temperature in a room. Try to avoid the use of electric fans when rooms are too warm. Check that windows can open.

Take action

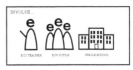

- Heat audit
- Heating system
- Energy loss foiled again
- Curtains to energy loss
- Dress to impress whole-school campaign
- Draught excluders supporting classroom lesson

Taking action on energy

Improving the space heating of the school may require costly structural improvements, but the Eco-Team and school users can still do their bit by monitoring room temperatures, optimising boiler settings, maximising heat output from radiators, blocking draughts and applying good practice in heating management. The heating policy, the practical actions, the involvement of the whole school and the monitoring and evaluating of projects ensure that the environmental management principles have been applied.

Project 1: heat audit

In the section *Getting started with energy management*, an overall energy audit of the school took place, but another audit can be undertaken with heating as the sole focus. This is more detailed and helps the Eco-Team begin to understand the school heating issue. The team will measure temperatures, identify draughts and identify where radiators are blocked by furniture.

- **Action 1. Eco-Team:** meet and plan.

  Look at the initial energy audit and where heating issues were identified. Plan how and when to conduct the heat audit.

- **Action 2. Eco-Teacher:** gather tools.

  Gather together the following resources:

  - Thermometers to measure room temperatures

  - Strips of tissue paper to identify draughts

  - Camera to provide photographic evidence

  - Heat audit worksheets, clipboards and pencils.

- **Action 3. Eco-Team:** carry out a heat audit.

  Visit each room in the school, building a profile of its heating arrangement. Pupils should:

  - Record room temperature.

  - Identify draughts from windows or doors.

  - Check radiators to see if they are on or if furniture is blocking them.

  - Check if reflective panels are fitted behind radiators.

  - Check pipes are insulated.

- **Action 4. Eco-Team:** analyse findings.

  After each room has been profiled, analyse the data and write a report.

- **Action 5. Eco-Team:** meet caretaker to report findings.

  Meet with the caretaker, go through the report and decide what action could be taken.

- **Action 6. Eco-Team:** contact local authority.

  The report can be submitted to the local authority with a request for help to implement measures, such as draught proofing windows.

Project 2: heating system

The Eco-Team can work with the caretaker to ensure the heating system operates as efficiently as possible. First, check that the boiler comes on at the right time and how long the rooms take to heat up. It could be that the boiler comes on unnecessarily early and therefore wastes energy. Then check the radiators to make sure they are at the correct setting, the thermostatic valves are tamper-proof and furniture is not blocking them.

- **Action 1. Eco-Teacher:** meet caretaker and discuss boiler settings.

  Arrange to meet the caretaker along with the Eco-Team. Ask the caretaker to help with recording temperatures in the morning as the school heats up. Provide thermometers for a sample area of the school to be measured.

- **Action 2. Caretaker:** record temperatures.

  The caretaker can measure and record temperatures across the school as the heating system kicks in. This will help build an understanding of how long it takes for the school to heat up.

- **Action 3. Eco-Pupils:** analyse findings.

  Analyse the recorded temperatures taken by the caretaker. Look at the temperatures at each time. Rooms should reach the correct temperature just as the users arrive.

- **Action 4. Eco-Team:** meet.

  Meet and discuss findings. If rooms are at the correct temperature as users arrive then no adjustment is needed; but if the school is warming too early, discuss what time the system could be switched on.

- **Action 5. Eco-Pupils:** check radiators.

  Following on from the heating system analysis, accompany the caretaker in checking radiator valves are set correctly and they are not blocked by furniture.

- **Action 6. Eco-Team:** rearrange furniture if necessary.

  If furniture is blocking radiators, discuss with classroom teachers whether room layout can be rearranged.

Project 3: energy loss foiled again

Silver foil reflects heat and so placing it behind radiators can help maximise the heat into a room. A simple set of resources can quickly improve heat performance.

- **Action 1. Eco-Team:** meet and plan.

  Reflective boards can help radiate heat back into a room rather than allowing the heat to escape through a wall. These can be bought in shops but they can also be made. Meet and plan to make the reflective boards.

- **Action 2. Eco-Pupils**: prepare resources.

  Count how many boards are required. Measure the radiators and decide how the reflective boards could be fixed behind them. Then the resources needed should be gathered. To make a reflective board, you need card, glue, rolls of silver foil, scissors.

- **Action 3. Eco-Pupils:** make foil boards.

  Spread glue over one side of the card. Cut the appropriate-sized piece of foil. Stick the foil onto the board and leave to dry.

- **Action 4. Eco-Pupils:** fit reflective boards.

  Visit each classroom and slide foil behind the radiators where possible.

Project 4: curtains to energy loss

During cold periods, make sure that curtains are closed at the end of the day. This can help reduce heat loss through windows as rooms warm up. The thicker the curtains, the more heat they will trap.

- **Action 1. Eco-Pupils:** curtain audit.

  Walk around the school noting which rooms don't have curtains.

- **Action 2. Eco-Pupils:** engage teachers.

  Visit classroom teachers and ask them to close the curtains at the end of the school day to help trap heat when the heating system comes on in the morning. Provide each classroom with curtains with a *Remember to draw the curtains* sign.

- **Action 3. Eco-Teacher:** request thick curtains.

  Ask the budget holder to buy thick curtains for all rooms, reminding them of the financial and carbon benefits to reducing space heating.

Project 5: dress to impress whole-school campaign

During cold periods, school users can be reminded of the need to dress appropriately. Rather than turn up radiators or switch on electric heaters (which are expensive to run and use a lot of energy), people should be encouraged to wear a warm top. See http://www.generationgreen.co.uk for a useful whole-school gathering and lesson plan on insulation and saving heat.

- **Action 1. Eco-Team:** investigate use of electric heaters.

  Conduct an investigation to see if electric heaters are used in the school during cold periods. Plan a campaign to avoid use of such appliances and have people wear appropriate clothing instead.

- **Action 2. Eco-Team:** meet and plan the campaign.

  Discuss the campaign, remembering to engage and encourage. A *dress to impress* day can encourage people to wear a warm jumper.

- **Action 3. Eco-Pupils:** engage pupils and staff.

  Make posters that remind people to dress warmly and avoid using electric heaters.

- **Action 4. Eco-Pupils:** encourage through the *dress to impress* competition.

   Have fun by running a competition to wear the best-looking jumper one day during winter. Pupils can judge which is best and a prize can be awarded.

Supporting classroom lesson: draught excluders

Each class can make draught excluders for its classroom door and windows. Extra excluders can be made for other parts of the school. See instructions in *Appendix 15*.

Water heating

Cleaning, food preparation, washing hands and making hot drinks all require the use of hot water. The heating of this water uses around 16% of the school's overall energy consumption[8] and so the successful implementation of the projects in this section can contribute to a worthwhile reduction in CO_2 emissions.

A hot water system in a building consists of a large number of pipes and taps and maintenance of these and the regulating of the hot water temperature are essential to reducing wasted hot water. The caretaker and the Eco-Team should start by working together to increase the effectiveness of the system by checking for leaks and drips and monitoring the hot water temperature.

Hot water management is about understanding how much energy demand there is, when it is demanded, how the water is used and then engaging with those who use it, including cleaners, caterers, staff and pupils, to agree and promote good housekeeping. A hot water policy based on agreements can be added to the energy policy as a commitment to best practice.

The Eco-Team can also help reduce hot water demand through several projects that include:

- Promoting effective use of water heating appliances such as kettles and dishwashers.
- Engaging with cleaners to discuss cold water cleaning.
- Meeting caterers and addressing hot water use in the kitchen.
- Running a whole-school campaign to remind people to turn off taps.

Remember

Health and safety should be considered at all times when working on hot water projects. People need to wash their hands in temperatures of at least 60°C, which is the temperature that kills bacteria. Always remind people to wash hands in water from the hot tap. Pipes carrying hot water can be hot so they should not be touched. A cold water cleaning policy can be agreed with cleaners. Discuss this with them and the local authority. Improvements to hot water systems can be technical involving changes to pipe-work. The caretaker and other technicians can be invited to review insulation and other possible measures. A water campaign can overlap with an energy campaign through the hot water theme. Be clear on the objectives for the hot water theme and remember that energy consumption is that which is being measured.

Take action

- Auditing
- What's hot investigation
- The science of hot water supporting classroom lesson
- Team time tales
- Cleaning with cold
- Kitchen clever
- Water wonders whole-school campaign.

Action on space and water heating can significantly lower the school's energy consumption, especially if structural improvements and maintenance checks are considered. The Eco-Team can play a significant role in setting up the routines and practices that allow for good management as well as engaging the pupils, staff, cleaners, kitchen staff and wider community in the campaigns.

Project 1: auditing

This project provides an audit of the efficiency of the water system by following pipe-work around the building and visiting toilets, looking for drips and leaks from pipes, radiators and taps. Make people aware that a leaking tap can waste around 5500 litres of water per year.[9] Also, monitor the temperature of the hot water and make sure it is not hotter than it needs to be.

- **Action 1. Eco-Team:** meet caretaker.

Meet the caretaker and make a plan to reduce water wastage. Ask for help to look for leaks and drips through the building and measuring the temperature of the water coming from hot water taps.

- **Action 2. Eco-Pupils:** gather resources.

    Gather the necessary resources to record findings – a previously used energy audit form or a piece of blank paper and pencil to note down where leaks and drips are identified. A thermometer will be needed for measuring hot water temperature.

- **Action 3. Eco-Pupils:** conduct audit.

    Conduct the audit, noting where leaks are and record how many taps are dripping. Try to turn off the tap to see if the drip is because it wasn't closed properly or if it is a broken tap. This information can be written up in a report and passed on to the school.

    At the same time, check the temperature of the water coming from each hot water tap. Let the water run for a few seconds and then hold the thermometer in the flow of water. Take a note of the reading. The water should be around 60°C.

- **Action 4. Eco-Pupils:** report findings.

    Present the findings about the drips, leaks and temperatures to the caretaker. These may be easily fixed. The caretaker can report back on the work needing done.

- **Action 5. Eco-Pupils:** engage whole school.

    Engage the whole school by launching a hot water saving campaign. Start by talking about the results of the audit and remind people to turn off taps. Explain that future projects will take place.

- **Action 6. Eco-Team:** daily checks.

    Aim to reduce drips by regularly checking that taps are turned off. This could be included in a set of daily eco-tasks.

Project 2: What's hot investigation

This project investigates the relationship between hot water and energy by taking electricity and gas meter readings before and after peak hot water demand times, such as break, lunch and after lunch when hands are washed, kettles are boiled and dish-washing takes place.

- **Action 1. Eco-Team:** discuss peak hot water demand.

  Discuss when and why hot water might be used at certain times of the day. Establish that demand may be higher at break times, lunch and after lunch. These times relate to washing hands when pupils go to the toilet, when kettles might be used to boil water and when caterers may be washing dishes. Plan to take meter readings to see the impact of these activities.

- **Action 2. Eco-Pupils:** take meter readings.

  Take electricity and gas meter readings directly before and directly after break. Do the same directly before and directly after lunch. Take another reading sometime after lunch to reflect the time dishes are washed. Repeat this over a few days to get a clear representation of hot water demand times.

- **Action 3. Eco-Team:** analyse meter readings.

  Calculate the amount of energy consumed over these periods by looking at the meter reading figures. This will show that hot water has an impact on energy consumption.

Supporting classroom lesson: the science of hot water

Encourage class teachers to use this lesson to promote the understanding that only boiling as much water as needed helps save energy. A kettle, water and a thermometer are required. Ask teachers to demonstrate how water heats up by boiling water in a kettle, explaining how energy heats the filament. Encourage pupils to measure out different amounts of water and time how long it takes to bring each amount to the boil. Discuss the different lengths of time and the related energy saving, explaining that only the amount of water needed should be boiled.

Project 3: team time tales

This project analyses how hot drinks are prepared in the staffroom. Staffrooms may have a water heater which may be on most of the day or perhaps the kettle is boiled with more water than is needed. Suggest best practice by boiling only as much as is needed and storing hot water in a thermos.

- **Action 1. Eco-Teacher:** scope behaviours.

  Conduct a scoping exercise by watching how water is boiled in the staffroom and kitchen. Observe and note practices.

- **Action 2. Eco-Teacher:** assess options.

  Assess options for best practice, including optimising the use of the water heater, using measuring jugs to fill the kettle, marking measurements on the kettle and using a thermos to store boiled water. Discuss these with the caretaker.

- **Action 3. Eco-Teacher:** implement.

  Implement the necessary actions.

Project 4: cleaning with cold

Cleaning with cold water is an option for reducing hot water demand. Debate exists over the effectiveness of cleaning products without hot water and so a discussion and agreement needs to be reached over the water temperature used to clean the school. A cleaning with cold water policy should be discussed with the local authority and cleaners.

- **Action 1. Eco-Teacher:** meet cleaners.

  Discuss with the cleaners how they use hot water. Assess if hot water is being used efficiently. Ask whether they have cleaned with cold water before. Reach an agreement to use less hot water where possible.

- **Action 2. Eco-Teacher:** seek guidance.

  Communicate with those responsible for school cleaning. Discuss the possibility of cleaning the school with cold water, explaining the financial and carbon savings.

Project 5: kitchen clever

This project is to work with caterers to monitor hot water usage and encourage best practice, making sure that dishwashers are full before they are switched on and that cleaning is done without wasting hot water.

- **Action 1. Eco-Team:** meet caterers.

  Hold a meeting with the caterer and discuss hot water use in the kitchen.

Explain the Eco-Team's project and ask if the team could watch how hot water is used in the kitchen.

- **Action 2. Eco-Team:** observe and assess.

  Observe how dishwashing machines are used and how cleaning the kitchen is done. Look out for potential improvements, such as making sure the dishwasher is full before it is used and look at how much hot water is needed to clean the kitchen after lunches.

- **Action 3. Eco-Team:** propose best practice.

  Meet with caterers again and compliment examples of good practice. Make any suggestions and recommendations based on the observations.

Project 6: water wonders whole-school campaign

This project engages the whole school in a campaign to minimise hot water wastage by turning off taps. It includes preparing a whole-school gathering talk, making reminder signs and rewarding positive behaviours. Parents can also be engaged with requests to reduce shower times at home.

- **Action 1. Eco-Team:** meet to discuss campaign.

  Start by meeting to discuss the whole-school campaign and planning when the actions will be implemented and who will do them.

- **Action 2. Eco-Pupils:** make signs.

  Make *Remember to save hot water* signs with pictures of taps being switched off. Put these up in toilets, the staffroom and kitchen.

- **Action 3. Eco-Team:** decide rewards.

  To encourage positive hot water behaviour, decide how you are going to reward individuals and classes.

- **Action 4. Eco-Team:** meet and prepare whole-school presentation.

  Plan a whole-school gathering presentation that engages the whole school in the need to reduce hot water waste, teaching why it is important. Explain the actions the Eco-Team has already taken and ask pupils to support the campaign by remembering to turn off taps and not to have water running for too long.

- **Action 5. Eco-Team:** letter to parents.

  Draft a letter to go home to parents asking them to join in the campaign. The letter should state the request to turn off taps and avoid leaks and drips as well as thinking about the length of showers. The website http://www. waterwise.org.uk offers suggestions and fun facts on domestic water use. Include a return slip to be signed and returned if the reader is going to take part in the campaign.

- **Action 6. Eco-Pupils:** deliver the whole-school talk.

  Deliver the presentation and issue each child in school with a letter to parents. Explain that those who pledge to take part should sign and return the letters.

- **Action 7. Whole school:** take action.

  All in the school should engage in the campaign taking necessary action.

- **Action 8. Eco-Pupils:** retrieve letter slips.

  Collect returned letter slips. Count them as these can be used as evidence of community engagement.

- **Action 9. Eco-Pupils:** record and share evidence.

  Update the eco-noticeboard with meter readings, number of people engaged in the campaign and other positive feedback. Don't forget to celebrate success.

Lighting

This chapter sets out the lighting projects that involve the Eco-Team in performing regular tasks and conducting a whole-school behaviour change campaign. An explanation of good practice in light management and lighting issues should help you prepare and launch a successful drive that saves not just energy but also money as lighting an average school accounts for 20% of its overall energy costs.[10]

School lighting consists of ceiling lights, desk lamps and lights in toilets, store-rooms and cupboards, and efficient use of all of these is what the Eco-Team should aim for. Some schools have modern lighting systems that include measures such as energy efficient bulbs, reflective panels and occupancy sensors that switch on the lights only when movement or body heat is detected and, thereby, avoiding the problem of people leaving lights switched on. These measures help to reduce energy use, but installing them usually requires investment from the local authority. No matter what type of lighting your school has, it still needs to be managed by the *monitor, control, conserve* approach.

The Eco-Team, by conducting spot checks and audits, can monitor the effectiveness of existing lighting while the caretaker can make sure lights are working as they should. Light levels are influenced by the amount of daylight outside, so by using blinds effectively, maximum use can be made of natural light.

Conserving lighting demand, meanwhile, is achieved by engaging the school users. There is often unnecessary light use in a school for example:

- Toilet lights may be left on.
- The staffroom may be lit when not in use.
- Teachers working in a room may have more lights on than is necessary.
- Store rooms or cupboards may have lights left on.
- The gym hall lights may take a while to come on so they are kept switched on all day.
- Cleaners may put on all the lights in a room when cleaning.
- Office staff may leave lights on after they leave.
- After-school clubs may use excessive lighting.

Shared responsibility is needed with everyone remembering to switch off lights when not in use. A written policy can help achieve this. High frequency areas such as corridors usually have lights left on for safety reasons, and appropriate lighting levels are needed in classrooms so there is no need to sit in the dark.

The actions the school and Eco-Team can take to run a good lighting management system include:

- Conducting an audit efficiency of existing bulbs.
- Fitting new low energy bulbs where possible.
- Cleaning windows to make best use of daylight.
- Teaching people to use blinds correctly.
- Scoping behaviours and identifying the opportunities to engage school users.

- Conducting a switch off campaign including making signs and labelling switches.
- Considering reflection and how it may be used instead of lighting.
- Engaging people at home by promoting better light habits.

Remember

Some people think that switching on a light uses up more energy than leaving it on, but this is not the case. Place *Switch off the light* signs on doors rather than by the light switch. If people are already looking at the light switch, they are likely to switch off the light anyway. Be aware of the light levels and avoid leaving people 'in the dark'. Good lighting is needed for health reasons. However, consider if all the lights need to be on in one room at one time, such as when only one person is in the room.

Frequently asked questions

Q: *Is it true that you won't be able to buy traditional bulbs soon?*
A: Yes. Traditional tungsten bulbs will no longer be sold in the EU after 2015.

Q: *Is it true that light from energy efficient bulbs is not as good as light from normal bulbs?*
A: No. Modern energy efficient bulbs provide light immediately and the light levels are equivalent to the old tungsten bulbs.

Q: *I've heard that low-energy bulbs contain mercury and are dangerous if they break.*
A: Energy efficient bulbs do contain mercury and, if a bulb breaks, take care with clearing the residue. However, the overall environmental benefit from low-energy bulbs vastly outweighs the negatives from the use of the mercury.

Take action

- Light audit
- Let the sunshine in
- Light reflection supporting classroom lesson
- Light monitors
- Switch on to switching off whole-school campaign.

Getting people into the habit of switching off lights and making the most of available light requires an understanding of their behaviours. Once this is understood, a set of systems can be more easily implemented.

Project 1: light audit

This project provides an audit for the lighting across the school by checking if lights are working and identifying where maintenance or replacement with low energy bulbs may be required. At the same time, it ensures all light switches are labelled clearly so that users will know which switch is for which light.

- **Action 1. Eco-Teacher:** teach Eco-Pupils.

  Teach the Eco-Pupils about the need to reduce light use, mentioning carbon and money. Explain that a lighting campaign will be launched, but before that the team must audit the lights in the school and take action to ensure a system of efficient light use by all school users.

- **Action 2. Eco-Team:** review the energy audit.

  Look at the original energy audit and focus on the section on lighting. Plan a more in-depth audit with a checklist of each light in the school. See *Appendix 16*.

- **Action 3. Eco-Team:** gather materials.

  Gather together the checklist, pencils and a clipboard.

- **Action 4. Eco-Team:** conduct the audit.

  Check that all the bulbs are working. Examine desk lamps and check that bulbs are low-energy types. Take care not to touch bulbs, as tungsten versions will be hot when they are on. Energy efficient bulbs give off little heat. Remember to list on the checklist where improvements may be needed.

- **Action 5. Eco-Pupils:** meet the caretaker and report.

  Give the caretaker the checklist to so that he or she can take forward any of the actions needed.

- **Action 6. Eco-Pupils:** label switches.

  Where rooms have more than one light switch, mark each with a sticky label to make it easy for users to know which switch operates which light.

Project 2: let the sunshine in

This project increases awareness of how to make full use of daylight so that lights do not need to be switched on unnecessarily. People sometimes use window blinds to block out sunshine to avoid glare; however, knowing how to use the blinds correctly and having clean windows helps to maximise the amount of daylight coming into the building and reducing the need for electric light.

- **Action 1. Eco-Team:** meet and plan.

  Meet and discuss the effect of daylight on electric light use and make a plan to have all the windows in the school cleaned. Consider who should do the cleaning, especially if the windows are too high to reach with a mop. Where windows are high these may need cleaned professionally.

- **Action 2. Eco-Team:** gather materials.

  Vinegar in water or eco-friendly cleaning sprays can be used. Use mops and sponges for cleaning and newspaper or cloths for drying the windows.

- **Action 3. Eco-Pupils:** clean ground floor windows.

  Armed with cleaning materials, the group can clean the ground floor windows from outside using a mop to reach higher spots. Tip: newspaper can be effective for drying windows without leaving streaks!

- **Action 4. Eco-Teacher:** encourage correct use of blinds.

  Daylight blinds can be effective in distributing light by reflecting it onto the ceiling. The blinds should be open slightly with the slats angled upwards and not blocking all the light coming in, as the diagram shows.

SUNLIGHT

REFLECTION

Using blinds effectively

- **Action 5. Eco-Pupils:** engage each classroom.

  Visit each classroom explaining the need for clean windows and the need to use blinds effectively. Demonstrate in each class how best to use the blinds, so that the room can be well lit on a bright day without glare problems and the need for electric lights. Each class can then be taught the *light reflection* lesson.

Supporting classroom lesson: light reflection

The aim of this lesson is to show that reflecting natural light can help reduce electric light demand. Gather together useful resources, for example: mirrors, old compact discs, foil (including washed, inside-out crisp packets), clear beads and sequins. You will also need wire or coat-hangers and pieces of wool.

Explain that the classroom can be made brighter using 'sun catchers'. Examine the different reflective materials by shining light on them or holding them in the sunlight. Decide which might be best to use to make a 'sun catcher'. In groups, take the wire or coat-hanger and attach the reflective materials with thread or wool.

Then experiment with a mirror or two on the wall. Does this help bounce light around the room? The Eco-Team can source mirrors and have them fixed to the wall.

Project 3: light monitors

In this exercise regular spot checks are conducted to ensure that lights are switched off in empty rooms during breaks and lunchtime. Once the system is embedded, the Eco-Team should prepare a rota and involve the whole school.

- **Action 1. Eco-Team:** take meter readings and check the electricity bill.

  At the beginning of the light campaign, take a note of the electricity meter readings for several days. Use this to compare with readings after the campaign is underway. Also, look at the last electricity bill and note the period the bill was from. Look at how many units were used. Compare this to the next bill and see if there is a difference in the units used.

- **Action 2. Eco-Team:** make a checklist.

  Make a checklist of all the rooms that are to be checked for lights being switched off.

- **Action 3. Eco-Pupils:** draw up a rota.

  Draw up a rota for who will check the rooms. Split into groups so that the rooms can be checked as quickly as possible during break and lunchtime.

- **Action 4. Eco-Pupils:** conduct checks.

  At the beginning of break and lunch, conduct spot checks in each room across the school. Split into several pairs, so that the rooms can be checked as quickly as possible. Assign each pair a set of rooms to visit. Note where lights have been switched off as these classes can be commended. Switch off any lights that have been left on.

- **Action 5. Eco-Pupils:** award points to classes.

  After the spot checks, analyse findings and award points or some other incentive to classes whose lights were switched off. Results can be announced at whole-school talks.

- **Action 6. Eco-Pupils:** extend rota to all the classes in school.

  Once the system for checking the lights is running smoothly, extend the rota to involve pupils from across the school.

- **Action 7. Eco-Pupils:** take meter reading measurement.

  Continue to take meter readings and see if there has been a difference in the amount of electricity consumed before and after the campaign. The electricity bill should also show the number of units consumed.

- **Action 8. Eco-Pupils:** share results.

  Share the findings with the rest of the school by placing meter readings on the eco-noticeboard and highlighting reductions. Celebrate this with the rest of the school.

Project 4: switch on to switching off whole-school campaign

This project involves making posters and signs to promote switching off lights when not needed. It requires engagement with the whole school and the message being taken home to parents.

- **Action 1. Eco-Pupils:** gather stickers.

  Switch off the light stickers can be obtained free from the Carbon Trust. Alternatively, the Eco-Team can make their own.

- **Action 2. Eco-Pupils:** plan a whole-school talk to launch the campaign.

  Plan a presentation to the whole school that explains that lights should be switched off when not needed. Be sure to mention the *light monitors* system of checking rooms at break and lunchtimes. Point out that if only one person is in a room then the light should not all be needed.

- **Action 3. Eco-Pupils:** deliver the presentation.

  Deliver the presentation to the whole school. Ask classes to make posters to remind people to switch off the lights and hold a competition for the best poster. Explain the *light monitors* rota and the points system or other incentives for classes that are found to be switching off their lights. Tell everyone to look out for *switch off the lights* stickers.

- **Action 4. Eco-Pupils:** put up stickers and posters.

  Place the stickers on doors so that they act as reminders to switch off. Collect the posters from the competition and award prizes for the best. Place them on walls around the school.

- **Action 5. Eco-Team:** write a policy.

  Write a policy on light use in school. Write that people should always switch off lights in an unoccupied room. Include the rule that if one person is in the room there should only be the appropriate number of lights on.

- **Action 6. Eco-Team:** meet cleaners.

  Arrange a meeting with the school cleaners and tell them about the campaign. Ask that they consider light use when cleaning and that they make sure to switch off lights in rooms once they have been cleaned.

- **Action 7. Eco-Team:** provide after-school club organisers with the policy.

  Speak to the people who run after-school clubs. Make them aware of the school policy on light use and ask that they follow the rules, using only the number of lights they need.

- **Action 8. Eco-Pupils:** engage parents.

  Write a short letter asking people at home to consider using energy-efficient bulbs and to switch off lights when they are not needed. Those who agree to take part in the campaign should send a reply noting their pledge.

- **Action 9. Eco-Pupils:** report and celebrate.

  Report on the success of the campaign, providing feedback to pupils, staff and parents. Highlight any financial savings as well as fuel savings.

Small power machines

Small power machines are the electrical appliances found all over the school. As a fun exercise, for one minute, write down as many of these as you can think of! You are likely to have come up with the following list: computers, monitors, printers, photocopiers, interactive boards, televisions, DVD players, radios, music systems, microwaves, toasters, kettles, telephone chargers, laminating machines and electrical fans. Remember the school kitchen where you find fridges, freezers, ovens and hobs. And don't forget vacuum cleaners, washing machines and tumble dryers too! Indeed, electricity consumption from household domestic appliances in the UK has shown an increase of 1.7% each year since 1970.[11]

With all these machines needing electrical power, a campaign that enables and encourages efficient use of these appliances can help you reduce electricity demand, which, on average, accounts for 3% of the total school's energy consumption and 5% of the energy bill.[12] Computers and monitors are the largest element of this demand because of the sheer number of them in a school, but catering equipment can also contribute significantly because fridges and freezers are switched on 24 hours a day. The campaign goal, then, is to promote the key best practice behaviours that require school users to:

- Always switch off computer monitors when they are not in use.
- Switch off appliances rather than place them on stand-by mode.
- Where possible, set *power down* functions on computers so that they turn off automatically.
- When purchasing new machines, buy low energy versions as they use less electricity.
- Ensure fridges and freezers are working efficiently.

With these behaviours as the target, the campaign can begin by teaching pupils about electricity. From there, the children can look at individual electrical appliances and investigate how different appliances consume different amounts of electricity. They will find that the highest consuming machines are kettles, cooking appliances and computer monitors. Knowing the wattage of each appliance aids understanding of the consumption and cost of powering each machine and, at this stage, pupils can learn how appliances are rated according to the amount of energy they consume. An 'A-rated' appliance is one that consumes the least energy while 'F' consumes more. Schools should always try to buy the highest rated appliance because they not only consume less energy but they are cheaper to run, which can help offset the cost of a more expensive version of the appliance.

The Eco-Team should then analyse people's behaviours, because inefficient appliance use is often down to people not knowing how to turn off an appliance or being unaware that stand-by mode consumes energy. To help overcome such barriers, the team can provide the necessary information and technical solutions to help people.

A small power machines management system includes the following actions:

- Regular spot checks of machines ensuring they are switched off when not in use.
- A project to fix appropriate settings on computers.
- Writing a best practice small power machine policy.
- Scheduling regular maintenance of machines such as photocopiers.
- Ensuring the green procurement policy includes small power machines.
- Engagement with all school users on best practice behaviours.

To create such a system, there are a number of key projects, tasks and actions that can be taken and certain behaviours to be encouraged, which include:

- Switching off appliances when not in use.
- Using a *power down* system.
- Teaching how to use each machine efficiently.
- Reviewing catering practices.
- Procurement of A-rated appliances.

Putting in place the management system, running various projects, promoting best practice and engaging with people through a whole-school and community campaign will help people to think about their own behaviours when they use machines and ensure a more effective and positive impact on the environment and electricity bills.

Remember

Inefficient use of photocopiers and printers wastes not only electricity but paper and ink as well.

Home energy monitors are small and measure and display the amount of electricity an appliance uses. These demonstrate how different appliances consume varying amounts of energy and can be a useful educational tool. Smart meters are high-tech and are replacing existing forms of gas and electricity meters.

In 2009 the average household owned 11 times more consumer electronics items than they had in 1970, and three and a half times more than in 1990.[13]

Frequently asked questions

Q: *Do screen savers actually save energy?*
A: Screen savers don't save energy. They may, in fact, use more energy than is needed.

Q: *Is it better to keep computers running, rather than keep switching on and off?*
A: No. Switch off computers when possible.

Q: *How much energy does stand-by mode use?*
A: It depends on the appliance – usually not very much, but get into the habit of powering down all machines.

Take action

- What watt
- Power-down plugs
- Power rangers
- *Say no to stand-by* whole-school campaign
- IT and energy efficiency supporting classroom lesson
- Care and repair
- Cook clever
- A-team.

The sheer number of small power machines in a school means that numerous opportunities to reduce electricity consumption exist. Create a system of good housekeeping and best environmental management practice by auditing the machines in the school and building awareness of those that are the highest consumers.

Project 1: what watt

This project investigates how appliances consume different levels of electricity. An audit of small power machines is conducted and an inventory recording wattage is written. Consumption is tested using a smart monitor, running costs are calculated and best practices for each item agreed.

- **Action 1. Eco-Teacher:** acquire a home energy monitor.

  Buy or borrow a home energy monitor in advance of the project. This will act as a useful educational tool. See http://www.itmustbegreen.co.uk/acatalog/energy_meters.html

- **Action 2. Eco-Team:** create an inventory.

  Create an inventory of all the small power machines in the school, taking careful note of how many computers and monitors there are. Look at the wattage of each appliance.

- **Action 3. Eco-Pupils:** learn about wattage.

  Gather together some small power machines and look again at the wattage of each (usually stamped on the item itself). Use the home energy monitor to see how each appliance consumes electricity. Note those machines that use the most.

- **Action 4. Eco-Team:** estimate usage and costs.

  With the information from the inventory, estimate how many hours a week each device is used and multiply this figure by the number of kilowatts (1000 watts). Now multiply this figure by the price of electricity (found on the school's electricity bill). Add together the cost of each device to get an estimated cost of running the small power machines in your school.

- **Action 5. Eco-Teacher:** agree best practice and write policy.

  Best practice for saving electricity from small power machine use is to switch them off when not in use. Include this in the energy policy.

- **Action 6. Eco-Pupils:** share information with school users.

  Make the calculations and policy available to school users before launching a whole-school campaign.

Project 2: power-down plugs

This project is one of the tools to reduce electricity consumption. Research the use of power-down adaptors for computing equipment. Join the 'Green Button' system (http://thegreenbuttoncampaign.com/) or consult the local education authority about a central system to shut down equipment automatically.

- **Action 1. Eco-Teacher:** contact the local education authority or energy department.

  Discuss the possibility of a system that automatically switches off the school's computers. Such a system powers down IT equipment at a set time of the day to avoid the risk of computers being left on overnight or at the weekend.

- **Action 2. Eco-Team:** meet and discuss the Green Button campaign.

  The Green Button is a Green IT power-saving schedule that automatically powers down the school's computers at times when they are not being used. See the Eco-Schools website.

- **Action 3. Eco-Teacher:** consult the IT department about the desktop power-down plugs.

Desktop power-down plugs are used to switch off equipment linked to a desktop computer. When a computer is switched off all the other appliances connected to the plug, such as the monitor and printer, will also switch off. Consult the IT department about buying these. Cost is around £5.00 at http://www.eonshop.co.uk.

- **Action 4. Eco-Pupils:** take meter readings.

  Before implementing these measures, note the daily electricity meter readings. Compare the readings with those at the end of the campaign to see how much electricity has been saved.

- **Action 5. Eco-Team:** implement the measures.

  Once the power-down measures have been agreed, put them in place to start saving electricity.

Project 3: power rangers

The Eco-Team conduct regular spot checks to make sure appliances are switched off when not in use.

- **Action 1. Eco-Team:** agree how to spot-check appliances.

  Look at the inventory of small power machines made earlier. Decide upon a method for checking that these are switched off and draw up a rota of who will do the checks and when.

- **Action 2. Eco-Pupils:** conduct checks.

  Form a *power rangers* team to carry out the checks. At break, lunch and home-time, check that appliances are switched off. Record where and when machines have been left on.

- **Action 3. Eco-Team:** analyse results.

  Look at the results of the spot-checks after one week. See if there is a pattern of machines being left on. Decide how to target a campaign that focuses on switching off those machines that are consistently left switched on.

- **Action 4. Eco-Team:** order supporting materials for a whole-school campaign.

  Obtain *switch off* stickers and posters from the Carbon Trust. Decide where these should be placed.

Project 4: *say no to stand-by* whole-school campaign

This is a behaviour change campaign that encourages all school users to turn off appliances when they are not in use. Daily spot checks are conducted and rewards are given out. The results are measured and the wider community engaged with and as many people as possible are involved.

- **Action 1. Eco-Pupils:** take meter readings.

  Note the electricity meter readings before launching the behaviour campaign.

- **Action 2. Eco-Team:** prepare presentation to the whole school.

  Prepare a presentation to the whole school. Make sure to mention the need to save electricity. Mention the energy saving measures that have been taken so far and that the next piece in the strategy is for people to improve their switch off habits. To involve people, launch a *switch off* poster competition. Offer a prize to those who make the best posters. Encourage people further by offering rewards based on the results of spot-checks.

- **Action 3. Eco-Pupils:** consider photocopiers and printers.

  Write signs to remind people to use the photocopiers and printers with care. Printing and copying should be carefully considered before use, so as to avoid mistakes and a consequent waste of energy paper and ink. Link this to the waste campaign.

- **Action 4. Eco-Pupils:** deliver presentation.

  Engage the whole school with the presentation.

- **Action 5. Eco-Pupils:** conduct spot checks.

  Conduct the daily spot checks.

- **Action 6. Eco-Pupils:** give rewards.

  Reward those classes and individuals that have switched off. Keep this going for at least a month until habits have formed.

- **Action 7. Eco-Pupils:** create rota for the school.

  Involve pupils across the school by allowing people other than the Eco-Pupils to carry out the spot checks. Draw up a rota.

- **Action 8. Eco-Team:** write a letter to parents.

  Engage the wider community by writing a letter to parents. Ask them to support the campaign by switching off appliances at home. Include a reply slip.

- **Action 9. Eco-Pupils:** count replies.

  The householders that respond to the campaign should return the reply slips from the letter. These can be counted and used as evidence of the number of people engaged in the campaign.

- **Action 10. Eco-Pupils:** inform the whole school.

  Keep the whole school informed by posting the meter readings and the number of people engaged in the campaign on the eco-noticeboard.

- **Action 11. Whole school:** celebrate.

  At the end of the month-long campaign, celebrate success by thanking all those that took part.

Supporting classroom lesson: IT and energy efficiency

The aim of this lesson is for all pupils to learn the energy efficiency settings on a computer.

Have pupils look up the energy saving settings on a computer. Demonstrate how to set them and let the pupils apply them to their computer.

Project 5: care and repair

Regularly maintained machines will operate better and are less likely to break down. The project includes consulting with the local education authority and energy department and setting dates for maintenance, as well as making people aware of how to report any faults, in particular with the photocopier and printers.

- **Action 1. Eco-Teacher:** agree a system to report faults.

  People should be aware of how faults with machinery should be reported. Consult with colleagues, the office staff and caretaker about reporting faults with machines. Agree on a reporting system.

- **Action 2. Eco-Teacher:** schedule maintenance.

  Contact the local education authority and ask about maintenance of small power machines. Fix dates for work to be completed.

Project 6: kitchen clever

Kitchen and catering is a major consumer of energy in a school. This project aims to encourage caterers to use best practice when cooking and storing food.

- **Action 1. Eco-Team**: learn about cooking and storing food.

  Be aware of best energy practice in cooking and storing food. Some best catering practices include:
  - Switching off equipment immediately after use.
  - Using appropriate-sized saucepans and boil only enough water as is necessary.
  - Keeping lids on pots and pans when heating food.
  - Switching off lights when not in use.
  - Filling the dishwasher completely before using.
  - Following best practice tips for fridges and freezers by:
    - keeping them around three quarters full
    - defrosting them regularly
    - making sure all the seals are good
    - standing them in a cool and well-ventilated area away from heat sources.

- **Action 2. Eco-Team:** consult caterers.

  Meet with caterers and ask about best energy practice in cooking and storing food. Explain that the Eco-Team could help assess where energy could potentially be saved. Agree best practice.

- **Action 3. Eco-Teacher:** meet with caterers regularly.

  Meet with the caterers regularly to continue discussing energy and waste issues.

Project 7: A-team

In this project, a policy is agreed on the green procurement of small power machines. A-rated appliances use less energy and therefore save money in the long run.

- **Action 1. Eco-Team:** review energy ratings of existing machines.

  Look at the inventory of machines in the school. Note those with high wattage. Investigate the efficiency ratings of alternative machines, taking note of makes and models. Make the list of alternative machines available to the business manager.

- **Action 2. Eco-Teacher:** review procurement policy.

  Meet the business manager and review the existing procurement policy. Agree on purchasing the most energy efficient machines in future.

- **Action 3. Eco-Teacher:** plan a strategy for replacing with A-rated appliances.

  When machines need to be replaced, make sure that the person responsible for buying the replacement is aware of the energy policy to procure energy efficient appliances. Provide them with the list of the most energy efficient alternatives.

Alternative and renewable energy

Renewable energy is a power source such as wind, solar or biomass (for example, wood chips), although ground source heat is often included in this list. This type of energy source can be generated through wind turbines, panels, special boilers or ground source heat pumps. All of these types of systems can potentially be installed in a school, but much depends on the physical suitability of your school site and, therefore, you will need surveys and investigations to be carried out. Also, costs of such systems may be prohibitive; but this section will help you to research the potential for your own school building and point you in the direction of potential funding support.

The benefits of installing a renewable form of energy, often called micro-generation, include reduced CO_2 emissions, cleaner air and even cheaper electricity for the school and/or local community. Installing such systems also provides educational opportunities for pupils, especially during consultation, design and installation when children can learn about solar or wind energy and look at the considerations for these types of systems. If installation is possible, a turbine or panel system can send out a powerful message about the school's commitment to the environment and help inspire the pupils. There is also the possibility of working with the local community through such projects, to bring about a mutually beneficial investment where the community shares in the benefits of the renewable energy, too.

A micro-generation system can be installed at any time but the best opportunities arise when a new boiler is to be fitted (biomass or ground source heat potential) or when a new school building is being designed. At that point consultation with the local council and community can take place, and there may be interested environmental groups or individuals. The Energy Savings Trust, Carbon Trust and the Low Carbon Partnership can assist with the process of advice, survey, networking and funding applications.

To achieve a renewable micro-generation project there are a number of steps to go through before it can be realised. These include the following actions:

- Research the suitability of your building by completing a questionnaire.
- Check that your school passes energy efficiency regulations.
- Have your school site surveyed.
- Consult the local authority regarding any necessary planning permissions.
- Contact local environmental groups about joint funding applications.
- Research funding channels and discuss costs with the local authority.

Follow these steps and, if it seems possible that micro-generation is an option for the school, begin to include pupils in the process of further investigation, looking into which type of system may be best. There is a list of useful resources, projects and actions set out in this section.

Resources

To aid the research and teaching of renewable energy and its potential in the school, several useful websites and resources exist in three different forms: advice, funding and teaching.

Advice

The Low Carbon Partnership – http://www.ourplanet.org.uk

The Carbon Trust – http://www.carbontrust.com/client-services/advice/public-sector-advice/expert-advice-for-schools
Carbon Leapfrog – http://www.carbonleapfrog.org

Funding

The FSE Group – http://www.thefsegroup.com
The Energy Savings Trust – http://www.energysavingtrust.org.uk/Communities

Teaching Renewable Energy

The Low Carbon Partnership – http://www.ourplanet.org.uk
British Gas – http://www.generationgreen.co.uk/resources/type/lesson-plan
Eco Style – http://www.ecostyle.co.uk
Energy for Educators – http://www.energyforeducators.org

Take action

INVOLVE...

ECO TEACHER   ECO PUPIL   WHOLE SCHOOL

- Investigation solar photo voltaic
- Investigation wind
- Investigation solar thermal
- Raising funds
- Making wind speed supporting classroom lesson

Project 1: investigation solar photo voltaic (PV)

In this project an investigation is conducted with pupils to find out if the school is suitable for a solar PV system. Note that a solar PV system may cost around £15,000 to install.[14]

- **Action 1. Eco-Teacher:** research.

  Read the Low Carbon Partnership website for more information on installing a solar PV system.

- **Action 2. Eco-Team:** investigate.

  Meet together to discuss solar PV panels for the school. Investigate the following criteria:

  - Is there a suitable south-facing roof or area of land?

- Is it free from shading?
- Will you need planning permission?

- **Action 3. Eco-Teacher:** seek further advice.

  If your answers are positive, contact the Low Carbon Partnership for advice on how to proceed.

Project 2: investigation wind

Here an investigation is conducted with pupils to find out if the school is suitable for a wind turbine system. The cost for a wind turbine system for a school usually starts from around £20,000.[15]

- **Action 1. Eco-Teacher:** research.

  Read about wind turbine options on the Low Carbon Partnership website.

- **Action 2. Eco-Teacher:** consider wind speed.

  The school site must have an appropriate amount of wind and to help you find out the amount of wind at your school, read the wind speed database at http://www.rensmart.com/Weather/BERR

- **Action 3. Eco-Team:** investigate potential.

  Meet together and carry out an investigation into the factors that affect wind turbine suitability. Explore the surroundings of the school, checking the following:
  - Are there surrounding buildings, trees or pylons?
  - Is there space to mount a mast?
  - Are there people living nearby who might be affected by the noise of a turbine?

- **Action 4. Eco-Teacher:** seek further advice.

  If the answers are positive, contact the Low Carbon Partnership for advice on how to proceed.

Project 3: investigation solar thermal

Solar thermal systems provide hot water through absorbent panels. Costs for larger systems, such as those installed for schools, commonly start from around £7,000[16] to install. Pupils can help to investigate the suitability for such a system.

- **Action 1. Eco-Teacher:** research.

  Read about solar thermal options on the Low Carbon Partnership website.

- **Action 2. Eco-Team:** investigate.

  Meet and start to investigate the potential for such a system. As with the solar PV investigation, check that the building is south-facing and free from shading.

- **Action 3. Eco-Teacher:** seek further advice.

  If the answers are positive, contact the Low Carbon Partnership for advice on how to proceed.

Project 4: raising funds

If a renewable energy system appears viable for your school, this project will help you to consult local community groups in order to assess the potential for joint applications to install a system.

- **Action 1. Eco-Teacher:** initial research.

  Visit the following websites to find potential funds and funding partners:

  http://www.grantnet.com/

  http://www.cdf.org.uk/content/funding-programmes

  http://www.communityfoundations.org.uk/community_foundations/map/

- **Action 2. Eco-Teacher:** contact other interested parties.

  Contact local community organisations and the local authority and ask about their interest in helping to fund a project.

- **Action 3. Whole school:** raising funds campaign.

  The whole school can get involved in raising funds for a micro-generation project and learning about renewable energy.

Supporting classroom lesson: measuring wind speed

To support learning about wind energy this lesson helps pupils to measure wind speed, an important element of the decision-making process, by making an anemometer. See *Appendix 17*.

End of chapter references

1 The Energy Savings Trust (2009), 'Schools: How to reduce carbon dioxide emissions from schools energy use'. NI186, London, p.1.

2,3,4 The Carbon Trust (2007), 'Schools: Learning to improve energy efficiency'. CTV019, London, p.4.

5 The Carbon Trust (2004), 'Energy saving fact sheet: Schools'. GIL147, London, p.1.

6 Department for Energy and Climate Change (2012), 'Energy consumption in the UK 2012'. London, p.1.

7 Department for Education and Skills (2007), 'Top tips to reduce energy in schools'. London, p.2.

8 The Carbon Trust (2007), 'Schools: Learning to improve energy efficiency'. CTV019, London, p.4.

9 Waterwise (2013), 'Frequently Asked Questions', Waterwise. Available from: http://www.waterwise.org.uk/pages/http://www.waterwise.org.uk/pages/faqs.html (Accessed 08/03/13).

10 The Carbon Trust (2007), 'Schools: Learning to improve energy efficiency'. CTV019, London, p.4.

11 Department of Energy and Climate Change, (2012), 'Energy consumption in the UK 2012' 12/289, London, p.1.

12 The Carbon Trust (2007), 'Schools: Learning to improve energy efficiency'. CTV019, London, p.4.

13 The Energy Savings Trust, (2011), 'The elephant in the living room'. CO325, London, p.23.

14 The Low Carbon Partnership, 2007, Products. Available from: http://www.tlcp.co.uk/products/solar_pv/types.html (Accessed 08/03/13).

15 The Low Carbon Partnership 2007, Products. Available from: http://www.tlcp.co.uk/products/wind/costs.html (Accessed 08/03/13).

16 The Low Carbon Partnership, 2007, Products. Available from: http://www.tlcp.co.uk/products/solar/types.html (Accessed 08/03/13).

Case studies

Case study 1: the 4 Es in practice – introducing composting

Flora Stevenson Primary School, Edinburgh

Behaviour change methodology can be seen through analysis of the approach taken by Edinburgh Primary School Flora Stevenson. Through the project on composting the 4 E model of *Enablement, Engagement, Exemplification and Encouragement* was put into practice when introducing the behavioural change of composting fruit waste.

Enabling the action

A compost bin and kitchen caddies were acquired from a local environmental organisation, meaning that the tools of enablement were in place. A few days later the organisation ran workshops on 'How to compost', which teachers and pupils attended; thus the information and knowledge were acquired.

Engaging people in the action

Pupils, parent helpers, an environmental educator and the local MP carried out an audit of the school waste. The school and the community were engaged in the activity because it was fun and relevant. After seeing the amount of waste for themselves, the whole school community got behind the campaign to reduce the amount of waste in school.

A whole-school gathering took place showing pictures of the waste audit to get everyone interested in reducing waste. The pupils were introduced to the compost bin and shown what they could put in the kitchen caddies.

The environmental educator ran workshops for all the classes in the school, teaching pupils how to make compost and boosting everyone's engagement in composting.

Exemplifying the action

The Eco-Pupils ran the composting scheme, exemplifying good environmental practice and setting an example to younger pupils in the school. The Eco-Teacher explained the new composting system to colleagues. She highlighted the school policy to achieve Eco-School status and that the success of the composting would help gain the eco-award.

Encouraging the action

For the first day of composting, every child who composted a fruit skin was rewarded with a sticker. This changed to a more manageable 'best composting class' of the week. The weight of waste going to the compost bin was recorded weekly and the figure placed on the eco-noticeboard and in the staffroom. Everyone in the school was encouraged by seeing the reduction in waste to landfill.

The school went on to achieve Eco-Schools status and they were complimented on their whole-school approach and their attention to monitoring school waste.

Case study 2: challenges and successful approaches

Rosendale Primary School, London

Rosendale Primary is a state school in south-east London with Eco-Schools status. A student-led school council and a supporting Eco-Teacher drove the approach to sustainability. There were successes as well as challenges along the way, and it is worth looking at the actions taken, the challenges that were faced and how barriers were overcome.

The main projects were to save electricity and gas and to introduce a recycling programme. The main actions the school took were as follows:

- Time was given to the Eco-Teacher (one morning per week) to work on actioning the school pupil council's eco-action plan.

- An analysis of electricity and gas usage from the previous year was conducted in order to create a benchmark to measure future actions against.
- Immediate action was for lights and projectors to be switched off during break and lunchtimes. Teachers who forgot to do this were named and shamed during assemblies.
- The large Victorian windows were taped up to help keep heat in.
- The caretaker was asked to switch heating off in classrooms when it was not needed.
- An investigation into solar-panelling for the school was launched, but upfront costs proved to be prohibitively expensive.
- Recycling experts were invited into school for workshops and assemblies to discuss the importance of recycling in school and sustainability.
- Each class was given a recycling bag and council members were responsible for disposing of the paper.
- An audit of recycling was undertaken once per half-term to ensure classes continued to recycle properly.
- Recycling boxes for batteries, printer cartridges, mobile telephones and board pens were located around the school. The school was paid for the volume of recycling collected by a third party.
- A wormery was purchased from cake sale proceeds. It was used to recycle some of the fruit eaten during break. A longer term plan was put in place to buy more wormeries to recycle kitchen waste.
- Ideas were floated to get a school pig and to feed it kitchen waste!

Successful approaches

- The head teacher took the initiative to tackle expenses, the amount of waste being generated and the general sustainability of the school.
- The student school council were given the sole remit for the year to tackle sustainability.
- The Eco-Pupils were provided with funding from the Parent Teacher Association and conducted their own fund-raising activities – the most effective being cake sales!
- The school council received 25% of all savings made over the course of one year to spend on whatever the council decided.

- Parents were extremely supportive and helpful.
- Lambeth Council were supportive.
- Children across the school were made aware of sustainability.
- Council members were aware of their daily responsibilities.
- Children took their learning home and helped change parents' habits.

Challenges

- School council members often failed to turn up to council meetings.
- School was tight for space, so there was no dedicated area for the council to meet.
- Classes were often not given the time to discuss council issues.
- Council members were not given the time to empty bins or monitor electricity use.
- Workshops were not rolled out across all year groups because of lack of time and other commitments.
- The central heating system broke during winter and electric fan heaters were installed for three weeks working 24 hours a day!
- Cleaners refused to dispose of certain rubbish.
- No periodical electricity or gas audits were taken to see if progress was being made.
- Initiatives became largely led by the Eco-Teacher as the children were not given enough time.
- The project became largely teacher driven with the children feeling they had lost ownership.
- It was difficult to promote a school-wide ethos on sustainability.
- Some classroom teachers had indifferent attitudes to sustainability.

The key learning from this case study is that success is achievable but expect there to be failures too. Providing time for pupils and the Eco-Teacher is crucial, and planning projects so that the whole school become involved is essential in order to create an ethos throughout the school. Being led from the top down, giving pupils responsibility, raising funds and seeing the benefits of actions were, however, central to the achievements and should be replicated in any school wishing to achieve sustainable success.

Case study 3: environmental management – putting theory into practice

Slim School, Germany

Slim School is a Service Children's Education school in Germany aiming for Eco-Schools status. Andrew Cunningham is science subject leader and was tasked with putting environmental management into practice. Here you can see how key elements of the discipline were met through an energy campaign, and where there were challenges.

The role of environmental manager (leading, facilitating and motivating)

I learned the Eco-Teacher role from previous experiences of running energy projects at previous schools but learned mostly by trial and error, rather than through any formal training. Leading projects was fun but finding enough time is challenging. It's difficult to give up lunch-times to have meetings, find missing eco-members, making sure they do their duties and organising a filler activity for them to do if I am away on a trip or off sick.

Also, another adult would have helped drive everything forward and made sure things went well. I just didn't have enough time.

I have also learnt, as an Eco-Teacher, it is important to reward the pupils for their help. I have handed out some small rewards, but bigger treats, such as a trip or an excursion, are better.

I have used my role to motivate and encourage the whole school, including colleagues, by introducing a system giving the class with the most eco-points at the end of week the 'Greenest Class of the Week' cup to keep for a week. Pupils are motivated and teachers too want to win and not get any embarrassing switch off *reminder slips.*

Parents were also encouraged to get involved by getting the children to take home switch off' *posters to be placed on the fridge.*

Pupil-led Eco-Team

I set up an 'Eco Warriors' team of eight children who had responsibility to play an active part in projects, such as designing posters, running competitions, checking lights were switched off and handing out reminder slips as well as keeping the eco-folder up to date. We drew up a rota of their tasks to make sure that all the 'warriors' were on duty the same amount of time and to give them ownership of the projects.

Tools

Useful tools I have used have been to learn from other schools, to draw on the experience of other leading science teachers, the Eco-Schools programme and the jointhepod internet resource. What also helped was having a keen and motivating head teacher.

Measuring and monitoring

The warriors monitor the amount of lights being used in school by checking how many lights are being left on in classrooms at break and lunch. We have timetables and rotas of who does what and when and the information is recorded regularly.

List of useful resources

Climate change

http://www.metoffice.gov.uk/education

Curriculum and education

http://www.sd-commission.org.uk/publications.php?id=879
http://sustainable-schools-alliance.org.uk/index.html
http://se-ed.co.uk/edu
Department for Children, Schools and Families, (2008) 'Planning a Sustainable School', DCSF, London

Environmental management

http://www.eco-schools.org.uk
http://www.ecoschoolsscotland.org
http://www.eco-schoolswales.org
http://www.eco-schoolsni.org
http://www.thinkleadership.org.uk/audit.cfm
Department for Children, Schools and Families, (2010), 'Road to Zero Carbon: Final Report of the Zero Carbon Task Force', DCSF, London

Footprinting

http://www.greenschools.net
http://www.educationscotland.gov.uk/schoolsglobalfootprint/about/approach tousingthecalculator.asp.
http://www.carbonpartners.org.uk
http://www.schoolsglobalfootprint09.pdf
http://www.energybenchmarking.co.uk/schools/default.asp
Sustainable Development Commission, (2008), 'Carbon Emissions from Schools: Where they arise and how to reduce them, SDC, London

Behaviour change

http://www.futerra.org.uk

Funding

http://www.fundinginformation.org/whatisfundinginformationabout.html
http://www.energysavingtrust.org.uk/funding
http://www.thefsegroup.com
http://www.energysavingtrust.org.uk/Communities
http://www.grantnet.com/
http://www.cdf.org.uk/content/funding-programmes
http://www.communityfoundations.org.uk/community_foundations/map/

Litter

http://www.keepbritaintidy.org/Expertise/Research/KnowledgeBanks
http://www.litteraction.org.uk
http://www.rspca.org.uk
Campaign to Protect Rural England (2008), 'How To Conduct a Whole School Litter Campaign', CPRE, London
http://www.mpsonline.org.uk
http://www.viddler.com/explore/ronansprake/videos/3/

Social media

Twitter
@1010
@EcoSchools
@Forum4theFuture
@globalactplan
@GreenAllianceUK
@neilgfraser1
@UKCEC

Waste

http://www.greenchoices.org/eco-shops/green-general-stores
http://www.ecoschoolsscotland.org

http://www.wastewatch.org.uk
http://www.recyclenow.com/schools/compost/index.html
http://www.gardenorganic.org.uk/organicgardening/schools-resources.php
www.sepa.org.uk
http://www.wrap.org.uk/
http://www.wastebuster.co.uk

Energy

http://www.carbontrust.com
http://www.cat.org.uk/index.tmpl?refer=index&init=1
http://www.carbondetectiveseurope.org
http://www.jointhepod.org
http://www.generationgreen.co.uk
http://www.create.org.uk/schools/teachers_resources.asp

Renewable energy

http://www.planlocal.org.uk/pages/videos
http://www.greenchoices.org/eco-shops/renewable-energy-suppliers
http://www.carbonleapfrog.org
http://www.carbontrust.com/client-services/advice/public-sector-advice/
expert-advice-for-schools
http://www.ourplanet.org.uk
http://www.generationgreen.co.uk/resources/type/lesson-plan
http://www.ecostyle.co.uk
http://www.energyforeducators.org

Tools

http://www.ecotoolsforschools.com
http://www.litterpickersdirect.com
http://www.amberol.co.uk
http://www.themebins.co.uk
http://www.treesforlife.org.uk/products/envelope_reuse_labels.php.
http://www.remarkable.co.uk
http://www.thegreenoffice.co.uk
http://www.ecostyle.co.uk/products.html
http://www.itmustbegreen.co.uk/acatalog/energy_meters.html
http://www.eonshop.co.uk

Appendix 1

Key sustainable behaviours

The main behaviours to encourage in school pupils include the following:

Litter behaviours

- Bring waste-free lunches.
- Place litter in bins inside school rather than the playground.
- Report litter dropping.

Waste behaviours

- Reuse paper on both sides.
- Compost fruit skins.
- Recycle all materials.
- Use only one hand towel when drying hands.
- Respect pens, pencils, books and other school materials.
- Choose appropriate amounts of food.
- Have a reusable water bottle.
- Avoid food waste by finishing food on the plate.

Energy behaviours

- Close doors and windows when heating is on.
- Report faulty appliances.
- Always switch off computer monitors.
- Switch off computers.
- Remind teachers to switch off smart boards.
- Only print when necessary.
- Switch off lights.

Appendix 2

Environmental review questions (litter, waste, energy)

Conduct a review of practices within the school to help you assess where projects should focus.

Litter

- Is there a litter policy already in place?
- Are snacks allowed to be taken into the playground?
- Does litter clearing by pupils take place on a daily basis?
- Is there a plan in place in how to reduce litter?
- Is the litter collected and weighed and results recorded?
- How many bins are in the playground? Is this sufficient?
- How much litter is in the school grounds? None, A little, A lot?
- Is the whole school involved in the litter reduction?
- Are there posters around the school promoting an anti-litter message?

Waste

- Is there a waste policy?
- Do waste audits take place?
- Is there a plan to reduce the amount of waste at school?
- Is there a paper recycling collection in place?
- Do pupils place paper in recycling bins around the school?
- Is paper reused?
- Does the school compost? Is it effective? How many compost bins are there?
- Is food waste monitored?
- Are caterers committed to reducing food waste?
- Are children encouraged to minimise food waste?

- Are inkjet cartridges, plastics, cardboard or other materials recycled?
- Does the school buy resources made from a recycled source?

Energy

- Is there an energy policy?
- Has an energy audit taken place?
- Are meter readings recorded regularly?
- Is the heating system timed?
- Do school users know how to report faulty appliances?
- Are low-energy light bulbs and fluorescent tubes used in school?
- Are the lights and whiteboards left on in the classrooms when people aren't in them?
- Are computers turned off when not in use?
- Are computer monitors always switched off?
- Is printing done only when absolutely necessary?
- Do people know how to use the photocopier efficiently?
- If it gets too hot in the classroom, is the heating thermostat turned down before opening a window?
- Is there someone in your school who has special responsibility for monitoring the consumption of energy in the school?

Appendix 3

4 E planning tool

Changing people's habits and behaviours is more likely to succeed if you have considered how to engage, enable, exemplify and encourage the action. A planning tool can help you.

Desired behaviour (e.g., for everyone to switch off computer monitors after use)	
Enable (How will you provide tools, knowledge or information to support the change?)	
Engage (How will you communicate your message?)	
Exemplify (How will you show this behaviour as normal? E.g., a policy that everyone must follow)	
Encourage (How will you incentivise people? E.g., a competition, routine checks and reminder slips)	

Appendix 4

Shrinking crisp packet lesson

Theme
Litter Reduction, Science

Objective
To learn how litter can be reused

Outcome
An understanding of litter's potential to be reused

Description
Take a plastic crisp packet and turn it into a key ring by shrinking it in an oven. The science behind the reaction can be explained.

What you need
Oven, plastic (not foil!) crisp packet (try a supermarket own brand or other cheap version), water, washing-up liquid, dish cloth, baking tray, foil, oven glove (for protection).

What to do
Discuss litter with pupils and how it is harmful to the environment and how, even when put in bins, it can be blown away and still end up as litter. List common types of litter found in and around schools (crisp packets!). Explain that litter is waste but it can be used for something else before it is thrown away. Suggest ways in which the material could be reused before being placed in a bin. Explain that a crisp packet can be made into a cool key ring!

- Preheat an oven to 250 degrees Celsius.
- Clean the crisp packet using water and washing-up liquid.

- Dry the crisp packet.
- Cover the bottom of the baking tray with foil.
- Put the crisp packet on the foil and put the baking tray in the oven.
- Leave the crisp packet for two to three minutes.
- Remove from the oven.

The crisp packet has shrunk!

This experiment will only work with plastic crisp packets, not foil ones. Plastic crisp packets are made from long chains of molecules called 'polymers'. In crisp packets, these polymer chains are stretched out straight.

When you heat up the crisp packet, the polymer chains start to get more energy. This makes the polymer chains vibrate and start curling up. The wrapper seems to shrink because all the polymer chains have curled up over each other.

Appendix 5

Litter art lesson

Theme
Litter Reduction, Art and Craft

Objective
To recognise that litter can have a second use as an artwork

Outcome
Create a piece of art using discarded waste objects

Description
Following a litter pick, use litter in a piece of artwork. Take inspiration from other artists and create a piece of art that reinforces the school's anti-litter campaign.

What you need
Safe and clean pieces of litter, internet websites for inspiration, glue, scissors, card or paper frames

What to do
Clean and sort litter collected from a recent litter-pick. Show these items to the pupils and discuss where the litter might have come from and who might have used it and begin to build a story of those items. Tell the pupils they are going to make a piece of art to reinforce an anti-litter message in school and the community.

Show images of litter on beaches, in the sea and harming wildlife. Now show inspirational litter art from websites such as:

- http://www.janerose.co.uk/gallery.html
- http://pinterest.com/museumoflitter/art-from-litter/
- http://www.flyintheface.com/exhibitions.html

Get pupils to choose items of litter and ask them to make pictures from it.

Use scissors for cutting up plastic and provide glue to stick pieces together. A glue gun may be required.

Finished works of art can be placed on paper and surrounded by a frame or displayed otherwise.

Appendix 6

Stop the drop campaign letter to parents

Dear Parents,

School Eco-Project – *Stop the Drop*

Help us to be Litter Heroes!

We are working to reduce litter in our community and we are asking for your help. Unwanted mail, sometimes called 'junk' mail, can be a source of waste and litter. Paper flyers, letters and envelopes sent by companies wishing to promote their products and services and promotional and local 'newspapers' are examples. To reduce this problem we would like to ask you to do four things:

1 For one week collect and weigh the amount of unwanted mail you receive. Let us know the amount you collected.
2 Place the enclosed sign, made by the pupils, asking for no promotional material on your letterbox.
3 Sign up to the 'Mail Preference System' which can reduce unwanted mail being sent by up to 90% – *www.mpsonline.org.uk*.
4 In one month we will ask you to collect and weigh your unwanted mail again and report the figure.

We hope these actions will help make a cleaner community, saving money and waste.

Thank you for helping and being a litter hero!

The Eco-Team

Appendix 7

Making recycled paper lesson

Theme
Waste and Recycling, Art and Craft

Objective
To demonstrate how the paper recycling process works.

Outcome
The children will have developed an understanding of the recycling process and how recycling is beneficial to the environment.

Description
Make a recycled piece of paper by cutting up used white paper and mixing it with water, then letting it dry to become a new piece of paper.

What you need
Used white paper, water, an electric mixer, a basin, wire gauze (net curtain stretched tightly over a frame can also work), thick drying cloths (J-cloths)

What to do
Begin the lesson by establishing the difference between virgin paper and recycled paper, explaining how trees are important and that recycling paper is preferable to sending it to landfill. Demonstrate the recycling process by following the procedures below:

- Rip up some used white paper.

- Place the pieces in a mixer with water – about as much as there is paper.

- Turn on the mixer until the paper has been chopped and blended with the water. The mixture becomes thick and porridge-like.

- Pour the mixture into a basin half filled with water.
- Lower a square piece of wire gauze horizontally into the mixture (pulp) and slowly bring it out so that the mixture is lying on top.
- Allow the water to drain.
- Turn the gauze upside down onto a drying cloth. Do this quickly so that the pulp stays on the gauze.
- Soak up the water using another cloth until the pulp is dry.
- Leave it to dry.
- Have pupils make their own pieces of paper by repeating the process.

Appendix 8

Paper raid lesson

Theme

Waste and Reusing

Objective

To encourage paper reuse

Outcome

The child will recognise an opportunity to reuse a piece of paper.

Description

Paper due to be recycled will instead be reused. Such paper will be put together using a plastic spine to form a notepad.

What you need:

Paper from a classroom recycling bin, a plastic spine (one for each pupil) or stapler, coloured pens and pencils

What to do:

Explain that recycling paper is good, but reusing gives things a second life.

- Collect paper recycling bins from around the school and take them to a central point, such as the classroom.
- The bins should be emptied onto the floor so that all the paper is easy to rummage through.
- Get the children to look through the paper and put aside good quality, A4 office paper that has only been used on one side.

- Each child should have a few reusable pieces of paper. They then lay the papers into a book with the usable piece of paper facing upwards.

- Attach the papers either with a plastic spine or by stapling down the side to create a book.

- The front page should be blank so that pupils can write *My Reused Paper Notebook* and draw pictures relating to the saving of paper.

Appendix 9

Card gift box lesson

Theme
Waste and Reuse, Art and Craft

Objective
To demonstrate the potential for reuse

Outcome
The child will have given a waste item a second life.

Description
Take a used card and by cutting, folding and gluing transform it into a box.

What you need
A used card (e.g., a Christmas card), pencil, ruler, scissors, glue

What to do
Give each pupil a card. Standard sized cards without any extra features (e.g., glitter, ribbons, holes) work best.

- Cut the card down the centre fold to give two pieces, one for the bottom of the box, the other as the lid.
- Using a rule and pencil, draw the template shape on the front page of the card.

A	B		A
Cut to line B			*Cut to line B*
A	B	B	A

- Using scissors, make four 'flaps' with incisions from the top edge of the card along line *A* until the intersection of line *B*.
- Now fold in the flaps.
- Press down on the edges to make a tight edge.
- The flaps can now be glued inwards to make a box shape.
- For the lid of the box, repeat the exact same process with the other piece of card.

Appendix 10

Compost in a bottle lesson

Theme
Recycling, Science

Objective
To deepen understanding of a natural recycling process

Outcome
The children will understand how compostable materials biodegrade.

Description
Create a mini-composter using a plastic bottle, soil, compost maker and natural waste and watch how it biodegrades.

What you need
A two-litre plastic bottle for each group of children, scissors, bag of compost, compostable material, compost maker (available from gardening stores), water, sticky tape, marker pen

What to do
Explain composting and its part in helping to reduce food waste going to landfill. Tell children they will see how compostable material breaks down or 'biodegrades'.

- Give each group an empty two-litre plastic bottle and help them to cut it open from a third of the way down the bottle so as to be able to place things in the bottle easily.
- Each group should first place a layer of compost at the bottom of the bottle.

- Then a layer of compostable 'wet' waste should be added (e.g., fruit skins, peels, apple cores).
- Add another layer of compost.
- Now add a layer of compostable 'dry' waste (e.g., shredded paper, card, leaves, grass).
- Repeat the process, adding layers of compostable waste including tea bags, coffee and eggshells.
- When the bottle is almost full, sprinkle some compost maker and a little water over the contents. This will act as a catalyst to the process.
- Attach the top part of the bottle using tape. Keep the lid on the bottle.
- Using the marker pen, draw a line marking the top of the contents of the bottle.
- Store the mini-composters in a safe place and over the next few weeks watch as the materials 'disappear' and the contents reduce.

Appendix 11

Egg packaging lesson

Theme
Recycling, Social Science

Objective
To consider effective ways of packaging goods with minimal packaging

Outcome
Children will understand that there are less wasteful options of products and packaging.

Description
Pupils will examine different types of packaging for the same product. They will compare multi-packs of crisps with large bags of crisps, cartons of juice with concentrated juice, biscuits wrapped individually with those in packs and create their own sustainable package.

What you need
Different versions of packaging for the following – juice (e.g., concentrated juice, cartons, cans, bottles), crisps (e.g., single bags, multi-packs, large bags), biscuits (e.g., individually-wrapped, multi-pack, packs with foil, packs with minimal packaging), fruit (e.g., loose, packaged), milk (e.g. small cartons, large bottles). Then eggs, scissors, tape, glue.

What to do
Give groups different packages to look at and compare:
- Small carton of juice versus concentrated juice bottle
- Multi-pack of crisps versus one large bag of crisps

- Individually wrapped biscuits versus packet of 'loose' biscuits
- Packaged fruit versus loose fruit
- Small milk carton versus large carton of milk.

Now lead a discussion on the purpose of each package and why they might differ. Explain that products with less packaging are less wasteful.

Provide groups with access to different packaging material, an egg and challenge them to make a package for an egg.

Test the design by dropping the packaged egg from a few centimetres above the desk.

Appendix 12

Making a pencil holder from a milk carton lesson

Theme

Packaging Reuse, Art and Craft

Objectives

To get children to realise that material often has a second use

Outcome

Make use of used milk cartons as a practical holder for pencils and pens.

Description

Use washed-out milk cartons by sticking four together for storing pencils and pens.

What you need

Waste school milk cartons (the type normally used for individual milk provided in schools), basins of water, dishtowels or drying cloths; enough for four per pupil, scissors, glue, paint and brushes

What to do

Ask pupils to wash out used milk cartons in the basins of water and then dry them using cloths.

- Each pupil takes four cartons and cuts off the top of each.
- On the back of each carton, smear glue and stick all four together in a square shape.
- Allow the glue to dry and, when ready, paint the cartons to make them more attractive.
- Use as a pencil and pen holder.

Appendix 13

Pledge leaf

Draw a leaf shape and write in the middle the following:

I pledge to reduce packaging waste by –

- using my own shopping bags
- choosing loose instead of packaged fruit and vegetables
- avoiding over-packaged goods.

Signed: ....

Give this to people to encourage them to reduce packaging waste.

Appendix 14

Energy audit questions

Walk around the school and answer the questions. The answers will help you understand how energy efficient the school is.

Note the electricity and gas meter readings.

Date:

Electricity _____   Gas_____

What is the floor area of the school?

Floor area _____m²

What time does the heating system come on and go off?

Time switched on _____

Time switches off _____

Are shelves fitted above radiators?

Are room temperatures more than 21 degree Celsius?

Are pipes insulated?

Are there any dripping taps or pipes?

Are windows and doors draughty? Note which ones.

Are outside doors closed?

Are lights on unnecessarily?

Are energy saving bulbs fitted?

Are computers switched off when not in use?

Are computer monitors switched off immediately after use?

Are there signs encouraging people to be energy conscious?

Is there a system for reporting mechanical faults?

Is there a water heater in the staff room? If so, how long is it switched on?

Appendix 15

Draught excluder lesson

Theme

Energy, Recycling, Art and Craft

Objective

To understand how heat escapes from buildings and to address heat loss in the school

Outcome

Awareness of school energy issues will be raised and active citizenship developed by tackling an environmental issue.

Description

Using an energy or heat audit as the basis for action, tackle heat loss from doors by making draught excluders.

What you need

One leg of an old pair of trousers or material 40cm long, fashion tape, an old pair of tights, stuffing (e.g., beanbag balls, rice, lentils)

What to do

Discuss how we use energy to produce heat and that it is important to use energy efficiently.

- Ask pupils where heat might escape from the school building. Mention that gaps at the bottom of doors are one such place. A draught excluder can combat this problem.
- Start making the excluder. Turn the material inside out so you have a long

cylinder that is open at both ends, with the 'prettier' side of the fabric on the outside. Stick together one of the ends using the fashion tape.

- Cut a leg off the tights and fill it with stuffing until nearly full then tie a knot in the end.
- Insert the stuffed tight into your draught excluder and tape the other end together.
- Place at the bottom of doors to prevent heat loss.

Appendix 16

Lighting checklist

Use the checklist table when conducting an audit of lights and bulbs in the school.

Light switch number	Room or area	Is the light switch labelled?	Is an energy efficient bulb fitted?	Action?
E.g. 1	Office	No need – desk lamp	No	Fit energy efficient bulb

Appendix 17

Measuring wind speed lesson

Theme
Renewable Energy, Science

Objective
To show how wind speed is measured and how this relates to producing wind energy

Outcome
The children will learn about the considerations for wind power.

Description
Make an anemometer to measure wind speed to help assess the suitability for wind energy at the school.

What you need
Four small polystyrene cups, marker pen, scissors, two same-sized pieces of corrugated cardboard, ruler, stapler, drawing pin, pencil with an eraser on the end, plasticine, stopwatch.

What to do
Discuss wind as an energy source. Mention how wind speed is an important factor.

- Explain that you are going to see if the school would be a suitable site for a wind turbine, by measuring wind speed by making and using an anemometer.
- Provide groups with the materials they need.

- Start by colouring one of the cups with a marker pen, as this will be necessary in measuring the wind speed.

- Place the corrugated card pieces in a cross. Staple where they cross over each other to hold them in place.

- Attach the cups at each end of the corrugated card cross by staple. Make sure the cups all point in the same direction.

- Now attach the cups and cross to the pencil with the eraser by pushing the drawing pin through the centre of the construction into the eraser. Push the sharp end of the pencil into the plasticine to form a firm base.

- You are now ready to place your anemometer outside in the wind, preferably placed as high as possible. As the cups spin, count how many times the coloured cup completes one revolution in one minute. This will give an approximate wind speed.

- Compare your findings with wind speed needed for wind turbines.

Index

The letter t following an entry denotes a table

Index